Marc Rivalland
on
Swing Trading

Marc Rivalland on Swing Trading

Marc Rivalland
on
Swing Trading

by

Marc Rivalland

HARRIMAN HOUSE LTD

43 Chapel Street
Petersfield
Hampshire
GU32 3DY
GREAT BRITAIN

Tel: +44 (0)1730 233870
Fax: +44 (0)1730 233880
email: enquiries@global-investor.com
web site: www.global-investor.com

First published in Great Britain in 2002

Copyright Harriman House Ltd

The right of Marc Rivalland to be identified as the author has been asserted
in accordance with the Copyright, Design and Patents Act 1988.

ISBN 1 897 59719 3

Printed and bound by Ashford Colour Press Ltd, Gosport, Hampshire.

For L and L-F

About the author

After graduating with a Bachelor of Commerce in 1975, Marc Rivalland was employed as a share analyst for one of South Africa's leading merchant banks. At the same time he undertook his Bachelor of Laws degree. In 1979 he emigrated to the UK and worked in the futures industry, first as an analyst and then as an account executive. He was team leader for Conticommodity on the LIFFE floor when it opened in September 1982. After a stint as a floor trader and arbitrageur, Marc was called to the English Bar by the Middle Temple in July 1987. He remains a practising barrister in the Chambers of Edward Faulks QC.

For 2 years Marc wrote educational articles on point & figure charts for London's Evening Standard. He also writes 'The Trader' column for *Investors Chronicle*, as well as giving seminars on technical analysis.

Updata charts

The charts used in this book were produced on 'Updata Technical Analyst', and reproduced with the permission of Updata plc.

Updata plc
Updata House
Old York Road
London
SW18 1TG

tel. 020 8874 4747
http://www.updata.co.uk

CONTENTS

PREFACE

Exploiting swings

One can tell from the great popularity of newspaper and magazine articles about obscure little companies that there are still hordes of investors out there trying to discover the next Cisco (before supernova). And a very worthwhile search it is too. Even though Cisco has fallen more than 80% from its highs, if you had invested £6,038 on the day it floated you'd be a millionaire today. This book will not help you do that for the following reasons:

• Swing trading is more about exploiting swings in share prices, both upswings and downswings, than trying to discover unperceived value.

• I imagine that some swing trading can be done in the little known, small capitalisation stocks which fascinate so many investors. However this book embraces a strictly chart-based approach to swing trading. Charts work best with well-known stocks which already enjoy high visibility and high volume.

Unearthing gems is no part of this book.

Why swing trade?

At the beginning of 2002, the financial press was trying to reassure investors that the FTSE was unlikely to go down, because it is statistically rare for it to fall 3 years in a row. As I write however (FTSE 100 = 4200), the FTSE will have to go up 19% in the second half of the year merely to breakeven. More than one Cassandra is suggesting that it has further to fall. If you're a long term buy and hold investor, what will you do? Probably nothing. That is what most investors do, persuading themselves that "It will all turn out all right, equities are a sound long term investment".

That may be true, but whereas many people think of 15 years as long-term, equities are a good investment only when you select a particularly lucrative phase (like 1982-1999) or when you measure returns over a period of more like 30-40 years. For example, adjusted for inflation, the Dow Jones peaked in 1966 and it went sideways or down for 16 years. It was the 1990s before it surpassed its 1966 highs on an inflation-adjusted basis, which means that those who invested near the peak in 1966 had a long wait for real returns.

What happens if the FTSE oscillates for a decade or more between about 3600 and its December 1999 highs of 6950? It is by no means impossible. By swing trading you can do something about it. You don't have to be a passive victim. I think of swing trading as the proactive way of approaching the markets.

There is not only a sound argument for swing trading. It is also exhilarating. I don't need to explain that. It's either true for you or it's not.

Swing charts and point & figure charts

Many traders already use charts as an integral part of their decision-making, and a good proportion of them will have heard of the particular trading method known as swing trading. Not many, however, know that there is a type of chart, a swing chart, which is tailor-made for swing trading, and even fewer will be actively using these swing charts. One of the main aims of this book is to introduce you to swing charts and to enable you to harness their power.

Some readers may be so convinced that they come to use swing charts as their primary tool. Others will prefer to stick to the charts they have used hitherto. I invite them to use the swing chart in conjunction with their existing techniques, or, at the very least, not to ignore the message conveyed by the swing chart. I use a combination of swing charts and point & figure charts.

For those whose swing trading depends more on value judgments than on charts, I offer this middle ground: if you must be led by a value judgment, why not use charts as a filter? Act only on value judgments when the share has a supportive chart; do not act on those value judgments when the share does not have a supportive chart. If your value judgment is correct, the chart is bound to reflect that in time.

Audience

I have my doubts whether the book will be wholly intelligible to those who have only a passing interest in the market. Recently, I tried to explain one of the simpler concepts to a legal colleague, but he professed total bewilderment (although I suspect him of brutish obstinacy). The book should appeal to a wide range of market participants and would-be participants.

a) Amateur Traders

There are private investors who come close to swing trading even though they don't know it. Take for example those who see a tip in a newspaper, buy the shares, and then, after the share price has gone up 20%, cannot resist bagging a profit. Unwittingly they have much in common with swing traders. They have exploited an upswing in price and, for whatever reason, have not held on in the way that a long term investor would. In addition, there are legions of private investors whose explicit intention it is to exploit price swings of various durations. This book should appeal to such swing traders.

b) Professionals Traders

This book is also suitable for professional traders, who could skip Chapter 1 and who probably know everything contained in Chapters 6 and 7 and most of what is contained in Chapter 10. Chapters 4 and 5 cover new ground the like of which has never, at least to my knowledge, been published before now.

c) Long Term Buy and Hold Investors

My publisher says I'm wasting my time trying to pitch to long term buy and hold (LTBH) investors. I know he's right, to an extent. Many people are simply too busy to devote time to the stock market, and many are too uninterested or daunted by it. It's true that if you don't know what you're doing, every decision you make is just an opportunity to make another mistake. Much better to make no decisions at all other than to drip-feed an amount from your monthly pay into a retirement fund. If you fall into this category, this book is not for you.

However it seems to me that there is a subset of reasonably active, market-oriented long-term investors who ought to read this book. Even if it doesn't persuade them to take up swing trading, it may persuade a few of them to look at a chart every now and then. If you are an LTBH investor, and you doubt the value of charts, consider the one below showing the collapse in Enron's share price. I've done it in point & figure format, but much the same comment would flow from a swing chart.

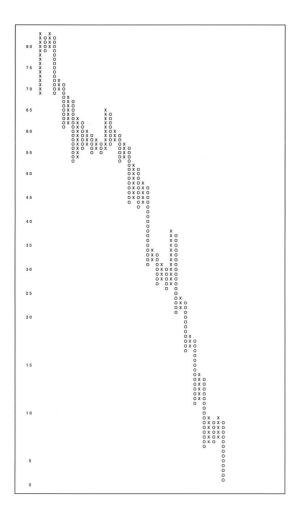

fig 0.1

After it peaked at over $80, Enron gave one buy signal at $58. As you will see from reading Chapter 7, that signal was the least trustworthy of all point & figure signals, and a sell signal was generated the next month (June 2001) at $53. Another sell signal, one of my favourites, occurred at $41, and other sell signals were given on the way down. At no time before reaching 12 cents did Enron give a buy signal. Need I say more?

In Chapter 11, I show how the occasional use of swing charts could assist LTBHs to hedge their holdings, to protect them from the sharp falls in the markets which have dismayed so many recently.

Structure of this book

The book is structured to cover my two favourite types of chart: the swing chart in Chapters 3 to 5 and the point & figure chart in Chapters 5 to 8. Chapter 9 explains how to use these charts together and Chapter 10 deals with the RSI. Chapter 11 covers LTBHs and Chapter 12 draws all the threads together.

The rather grand title of this book may suggest to some that I consider myself a 'guru' in this subject. Nothing could be further from the truth. My publisher's motive in choosing that title was to make it plain that the book is my subjective view of certain aspects of charting technique and interpretation, rather than a distillation of well-worn rules. The book can't cover everything I know, but I believe it does cover the most important techniques to enable you to make money out of swing trading.

I hope the book provokes thought. Any constructive criticism or ideas can be sent to me by email at info@marcrivalland.com or at m.rivalland@no1serjeantsinn.com.

1 INTRODUCTION

- Early lessons

- What is a swing trade?

- What is the point of swing trading?

- What makes a swing trader?

- Who swing trades?

- Swing trading and charts

- The logic underlying the use of charts

Early lessons

From an early age I was fascinated by how bad my father and his acquaintances were when it came to investing in the stock market. I remember listening to the radio with my father as we marked off the closing prices in a jotter or on a newspaper. I seem to remember most of the news being adverse. Resigned disgruntlement seemed to be the order of most days. But when there was an upward run, well … transports of delight. Midas had competition. My father had known it all the time. That idiot market had been wrong, as it so often was, but now it was starting to get the hang of things. There was still a faint hint of disappointment that more of the particular wonder stock had not been purchased.

In time he gave up, and concentrated on making money in something that he was skilled at. But he, and almost every adult I met in the late 1960s and early 1970s, had tales to relate of an occasional exciting financial killing, interspersed with considerable woe. They were very clear that stock market speculation was only for insiders and fools, and that it was impossible to make money out of the market other than by buying a mutual fund and leaving the money there for a lifetime. As a rebellious adolescent with the usual contrarian instincts, it seemed to me that they must be wrong.

I decided to do a first degree in commerce to learn all about the stock market and to find out what made it tick. I saw my first point & figure chart in 1973, my freshman year at University. It electrified me, and, judging from the letters to the newspaper, it roused considerable public interest. But I had studies to attend to. A couple of years later I did manage to obtain, almost by accident, a copy of A.W. Cohen's seminal work on point & figure charting[1].

After graduating I decided to do my law degree part-time so that I could get a job with a merchant bank and further my understanding of the stock market. A few months later, filled with the confidence of youth, I bought my first share, Tedelex, a manufacturer of televisions. In the repressed South Africa of the 1950s and 1960s it was thought that television would corrupt the morals of the people. Later on the government relented. Most South Africans saw their first television broadcast in about 1973. In mid-1976, as I was working in the research department of the merchant bank, Tedelex was due to report its results. It was a small company which had managed to secure one of only five (I think) licenses to manufacture/assemble televisions. Our research department expected its profits to rise over 200%. We were all standing over the ticker when the news came out that profits had in fact increased 600%. Nearly everyone in the office immediately bought the shares.

What is more, I bought far more than I could afford, on margin, because this was, after all, a sure thing. And so it proved, momentarily. The shares ticked up, then down, then up again. It seemed as if every fourth or fifth trade crossing the tape was Tedelex. Even the old hands had never seen anything like it. By the end of the day, on record volume, the share price was down about 1% from my purchase price. Nothing to worry about, save that my manager was peering at the ticker with a grim expression on his face. It's churning, he said. He explained that there

---

1. *How to Use the 3-point Reversal Method of Point & Figure Stock Market Trading* by A.W. Cohen (Chartcraft Inc.1947)

was too much selling. I didn't understand that at all. There was just as much buying, so it seemed to me. He sold out the next day. I held on and naturally lost a lot.

• It was my first real time lesson in the message which price action delivers. In a bull market, expanding volume makes prices go up. If it doesn't, question your premise. Perhaps the bull market has ended or is about to.

What is a swing trade?

Unlike day trading or long-term investing, swing trading is not a well-defined term. Broadly, it fits between day trading and long-term investing, in terms of time horizon and in other respects. A definition which I find useful is:

A swing trade is one which seeks to capitalise on the short-term downswings and upswings in share prices.

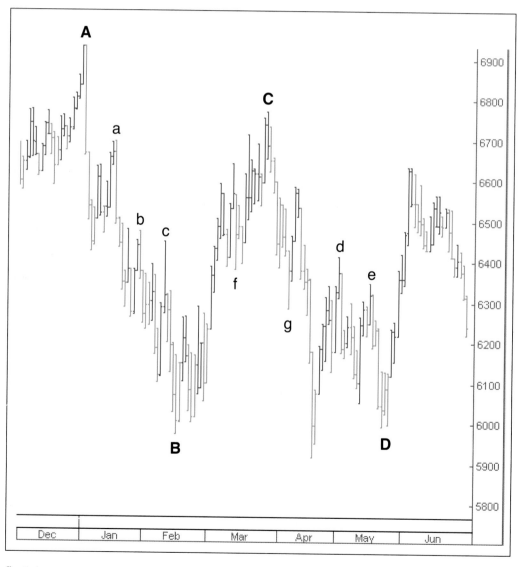

fig 1.1

You can see from the chart opposite that the FTSE moved from a high of 6950 on 30th December 1999 down to a low of 5973 on 15th February 2000, a move of 970 points (13.9%) in 6 weeks. Thereafter it moved up, virtually in a straight line, to 6770 by 27th March 2000, a move of nearly 800 points (13.3%) in just short of 6 weeks. Those two swings accounted for 1770 FTSE points or the equivalent of a return of over 27% in just 3 months. Yet somebody who bought and held a basket of stocks similar to that in the FTSE 100 index would have been showing a loss of 180 points (2.5%) on the 27th March 2000 when compared to 30th December 1999.

The broad swings were:

• down from point A to point B
• up from point B to point C
• down from point C to point D

The swing trader attempts to profit from each of those swings, which plainly represented the short-term trend of the market. But within those broad swings there were many lesser swings which amounted to corrections (brief movement counter to the trend) which also provided attractive opportunities to the swing trader. So an aggressive swing trader would aim to sell short at points a, b, c, d and e, and to go long at points f and g.

In this book, I use the term 'swing' interchangeably to refer to the broad swings and to the lesser mini-swings. It should be obvious from the context what I am referring to, and even if it isn't, I doubt whether it will make much difference to the point I will be trying to make.

Short-term trends tend to last about 4 to 16 weeks. That is the time horizon of the swing trader. Plainly it differs from the time horizon of the long-term buy and hold investor.

But it is not only time horizon which separates the swing trader from the buy and hold investor. Their attitudes to adversity differ fundamentally. The buy and hold investor will ride out downturns in the market in the confidence that his stock purchases were made at 'rational' prices and that the market will, in due course, reflect the full value of the shares. From this point of view, a market downturn may be an opportunity to buy more shares below their true value and to profit when they recover. Warren Buffett, the ultimate LTBH investor, expressed this approach most eloquently when asked by Forbes magazine in 1974 how he felt about the bear market:

"Like an oversexed guy in a harem. This is the time to start investing."

But until the LTBH investor thinks it is time to "start investing", he will bear his paper losses with apparent stoicism.

By contrast, the swing trader will admit defeat when the market moves against him and he will alter his trading stance to take advantage of the newly perceived market direction.

What is the point of swing trading?

Why bother, you may ask. Why not try to emulate Warren Buffett, who has not done badly to say the least. Why not re-balance one's portfolio once or twice a year and sit back and watch the money roll in. Well, it is perfectly true that the 18 year bull market from 1982 onwards gave investors a relatively easy ride, and has altered, for the worse I suspect, their approach to the markets. Putting money in the markets has been a sure thing, until the last 2 years.

Reverting to the above chart: although the buy and hold investor might have consoled himself in late March 2000 that he was only 2.5% worse off than at the beginning of the year, the truth of the matter was that the year had already provided two glorious trading opportunities for the swing trader to make a killing. Being 'not much worse off' in March 2000 amounted to a waste of one of the few easy phases to make money which the market presents. When the stock market finished the year at 6222, another 8.1% down from the highs of March 2000, the long term buy and hold investor could only hope for better times, which, so far, have not materialised.

Why should a market which goes broadly sideways or down imprison one's capital? Trading the swings is not only fun, it is profitable. 2000 and 2001 were good years for swing traders, and I don't mean only because they fared better than buy and hold investors. What I mean is that the charts had several clear swings with consistent and profitable chart signals.

You may say: so what? This is a post-bubble pause. Normal service will be resumed, and making money by armchair investing will once again become easy. That may happen. But what if it doesn't?

I have already mentioned the 16 year period between 1966 and 1982 as a leading example of share price stagnation. It is not the only example. After the 1937 highs, it took the Dow 8 years to make new highs, and those were still well below the 1929 highs. Those who bought shares near the top in 1929 had a 25 year wait for new highs in the Dow.

Finally I suppose swing trading is, to some extent, born out of leverage, at least for the private investor. The ability to buy futures, options and contracts for a difference means that trading a broad swing successfully can yield substantial profits, out of proportion to the capital employed. W.D. Gann said:

"A study of swings in active stocks will convince a man that he can make far greater profits in swings than in any other way of trading."

However true that may be, please note that Gann was not suggesting that long-term investing is less profitable. He didn't address that issue at all. Of course buy and hold can be more rewarding than swing trading in certain market conditions. I am certainly not suggesting that swing trading is the only way to approach the markets. But unless (and even if) you foresee another long and sustained bull market of the type that happened in the period 1982 to 1999, swing trading does have much to commend it.

What makes a swing trader?

Swing trading is not something to be undertaken lightly. Anyone who enjoys and is good at playing cards, particularly a game like bridge, should be a good swing trader. The same skills are used, namely drawing inferences from incomplete information.

But whether or not you like playing cards, swing trading needs more than ability. Shortly after I started writing about point & figure charts for the *Evening Standard*, my head of chambers Edward Faulks QC approached me and said "Catherine and I sat down last night to read one of your articles but I'm afraid we could make no sense of it at all". Of course, it was just a tease. If Edward had been briefed in a case involving point & figure charting he would have mastered his brief within days and he would have been ready to cross-examine an expert on the subject.

The true message was that he was not sufficiently interested in speculating on the stock market. No doubt he owns shares, but trading in and out of them is not something that fires his imagination. On the other hand, I am and always will be gripped by price action. To be a swing trader, you need to love playing the markets.

Who swing trades?

There is an army of short-term private investors who are trading swings, even though some may not realise it. Anyone who is not intending to open and close a position in a day or so, nor intending to ride out whatever valleys may be encountered, is attempting to capitalise on a favourable swing. Indeed, in part, this book is aimed at those who have the ethos of the swing trader (in that they bag a good profit when they see one) but who may not have made clear to themselves a method for repeating their successes.

In addition, much hedge fund trading is effectively swing trading. The same is true of proprietary trading by investment houses.

Swing trading and charts

Many swing traders are avid users of charts. Some swing traders, although they decry the use of charts, draw inferences from sentiment indicators and use the price action of the market or a particular security to time their entries, which to my mind means they use similar skills to the chartist. It is possible to swing trade without using a chart at all, but I'm not sure how successful it would be. At any rate I wouldn't attempt it.

Last year I gave a talk to a private investment club of about 10 members. They were struggling. They had made money in the technology media and telecom sector as it stormed up until March 2000. They had prudently sold out at the first sign of trouble and even more prudently they had had the discipline not to dive back into the sector for about 6 months. But the temptation had become too great to resist. They showed me 7 purchases they had made and invited me to comment on where they had gone wrong. They did not use charts at all.

To my astonishment, every single purchase had been timed excellently. Within days of each purchase they were showing profits. It was plain on analysis what they were doing. They were catching falling knives. They had chosen well-respected companies. And each time that company took a battering which appeared overdone, they leapt into the stock. Their judgment was rewarded when the stock bounced, sometimes over a period of several weeks. They were making a value judgment, and the market confirmed, temporarily, their beliefs. When the stock later fell below their purchase level, it must have seemed as if another bargain was on offer. In two cases, they did add to a losing position, which at least had the virtue of logic, although it would be anathema to a swing trader.

Effectively they were failing to take their profits quickly enough. Their profit expectations were more aligned with their previous happy experience. But they did prove that it is possible to use purely value judgments to initiate swing trades.

The trouble is, value judgments are subjective, and if they are not shared by the rest of the market participants, you will suffer losses. Losses arising from value judgments can be bewildering, annoying and most importantly, discouraging. Like my father, you cannot understand why this dunderhead of a market has got it so wrong. Of course the chartist also suffers losses, but they are entirely explicable, and although they are not to be welcomed, once you become case-hardened they are not discouraging. I suspect too, although I cannot prove it, that the size of the loss suffered by the chartist on each transaction is much smaller than that suffered by the non-chartist.

I commend the use of charts. Indeed although I have in the past made precisely the same mistake of catching falling knives, I would no longer dream of doing what that investment club did. If you have a full-time job, it seems to me the playing field is not level if you base your decisions on value judgments. The leading banks and brokers have legions of highly paid, highly trained investment analysts to research companies and to work out the value of a stock. When you, a private investor, buy a well-known stock based on your own value judgments, you are impliedly suggesting that the market, or those analysts, have got it wrong or in some way they have missed a trick. That seems like a pretty bold idea when you are devoting the majority of your time to pursuits other than the market.

This book will put forward a disciplined way of swing trading. You will not have the thrill experienced by the aforementioned investment club of seeing your value judgments almost instantly rewarded, because you will not buy stocks in a downtrend, however cheap they may seem. Cheap and expensive will not be part of your lexicon.

On the other hand, you will not suffer the same losses as the investment club. Of course, you will suffer some losses, but you will feel in control. Your losses will not paralyse you. You will have insight into both profits and losses and, to paraphase Kipling, you will treat those two imposters the same (no, not really, but you will at least be sanguine about losses).

No doubt there are a few canny investors who are able to trade swings based purely on their reading of the mood of the market, but it is a rare (and, I suspect, transient) skill. Sentiment indicators are successfully based on the very idea that the majority are overly bullish at the highs and overly bearish at the low.

My approach to swing trading is purely as a chartist. When you use a chart at least you get to see a picture which sums up the judgments, beliefs and expectations of all the market participants. It seems to me that not to use a chart is deliberately to give up a useful piece of information.

Of course, since I read and view the financial news, I can hardly avoid having an opinion on the present and future state of the economy, but I try to suppress these opinions. Analysing swing charts, point & figure charts and using the tools I enlarge upon in this book means that you need never take any meaningful account of fundamental information again. Your value judgments will be a backdrop to your trading, but they will not mislead you in the way that they so often do. Of course if you prefer to use fundamental information in addition to charts, that is a matter for you.

The logic underlying the use of charts

Here I intend to be brief. My publisher has rightly told me not to bore readers by indulging in lengthy academic discussion, and defending the use of charts is something that has come to exhaust me. Too many people, including some very bright friends of mine, have an obdurate visceral response to charts. I am convinced it is because they elect not to think in this respect.

Perhaps their minds close because they fail to realise just how limited and modest are the claims of the thinking chartist. For example:

> • All chartists accept that the chart describes past price action, the relevance of which may yield to future events.

> • No-one sensible suggests that charts foretell the future. The chartist accepts this limitation, but since second sight is not yet commercially available, there are not too many alternatives.

> • When an unforeseeable event occurs, it was not 'foreseen' in any way by the chart. It is pure coincidence if a disastrous event occurs in the middle of a bear market.

> • Point & figure charts and swing charts do not predict what will happen to the share price. They merely portray an imbalance of supply and demand which it is *assumed* is likely to continue until a new balance is found.

• Charts do *not* work because a pattern which occurred in the past is occurring again. That is just the sort of nonsense that makes people dubious about charting. It has nothing to do with history repeating itself. How could it? Everyone knows history does not replicate itself exactly (same demographics, same climate, same product, same demand, same supply). Broad themes may repeat themselves, but that's about it.

A chart is simply a pictorial representation of the forces of supply and demand. Those forces are not static. What makes share prices move? It is disequilibrium. If there were exact equilibrium between buyers and sellers of a share, the price would stand still.

Of course exact equilibrium is of no interest. It is periods of broad equilibrium which are most revealing. When buyers step in to reverse a fall in price, one can infer that the dominating view of the market is that the shares are cheap at that point. When sellers or buyers dominate repeatedly at the same level, a relevant inference may be drawn. The battle lines between the forces of supply and demand emerge. When one side is overwhelmed, you will see it in the chart. Join the winners.

Naturally future events are going to have an impact upon the share price. But the process of finding a new equilibrium, either higher or lower, tends to be an evolving one. Take a look, for example, at *Investors Chronicle*. Each week it publishes the views of various brokers and investment houses on a particular share. Usually three different views are given. Quite often the views cover the entire spectrum. One brokers says buy, the other broker says hold, and the third says sell. What do you think happens when the price starts going up? The clients and/or followers of the broker who said buy are filled with confidence, and may buy more. The clients and/or followers of the broker who said sell are filled with doubt. If they are short they may look to cover. If they are not short or if they are underweight they may look to re-balance their portfolios. The pressure to do so grows as the price advances. And so it is seen that apart from shock announcements, prices adjust by a process of evolution, not by step-change.

It is that evolutionary process which the chartist is relying upon when he acts on a buy or sell signal. He trusts the forces of demand (or supply) which have just won a battle to keep winning battles until the market arrives at a new consensus about the value of a share.

Of course sometimes when one has drawn a proper inference from a bullish looking chart, and bought the share, a future event such as a profit warning will happen that will crush the share price. That doesn't mean that the chart is useless or invalid. The chart is bound to produce some losses. What one is trying to do with the chart is to improve one's chances by drawing the best inference that one can about likely future price movement from an impeccable (but not clairvoyant) source - the current picture of supply and demand.

2 SWING TRADING IN PRACTICE

- Selling short

- Normal service

- Linear phases and how to spot them

- My approach

- The tooled-up swing trader

Selling short

It is a fundamental part of swing trading to sell short. Whereas the buy and hold investor purses his lips when prices start to fall, it's a matter of jubilation for swing traders. Why jubilation? *Because the market is at its easiest when prices fall.* A.W. Cohen, father of point & figure charting, calculated that prices fall almost twice as fast as they rise. It is surely within everyone's experience that prices fall much faster than they rise. You can see it in almost every chart you look at. Prices rise in a measured, steady fashion, then there is a bout of hesitancy, or perhaps a piece of bad news which causes the market to sell off, then the market regroups and advances cautiously. Occasionally there are bursts of irrational exuberance. By contrast when prices fall, it's one way traffic. Institutions (and no doubt other traders and investors) head for the exits. There is little hesitancy. Self-preservation is the keynote.

Recently I was stunned to receive an e-mail by way of feedback from a speech I had made. The delegate said that I had "given him the courage to go short". Good grief. I hope he was young, otherwise life has passed him by. If you think my enthusiasm for selling short is a product of the market's behaviour over the past 2 years, you're mistaken. The bear market in 1994 and the short-term downtrends in 1997 and 1998 are great examples of the money-making opportunities provided by a falling market.

Selling short is always talked about in the press as something wild and dangerous to do. And the press like to portray it as faintly scandalous to sell something that you don't own. I've never quite understood that, probably because my second job was in the commodity markets. Selling a contract was merely the making of a promise to deliver a commodity whilst buying a contract was merely a promise to accept delivery of a commodity. These delivery-related promises had nothing of the flavour of the anti-social that one might sell something that one doesn't own.

Selling short is not dangerous, except in certain limited respects. For example, in commodities, a weather-related crisis may cause orange juice futures or coffee futures to lock limit up for days. Answer: don't short commodities. Let someone else make money that way.

As for shorting equity indices, I perceive virtually no intrinsic danger at all. One's potential losses seem no greater than being long the market. If anything, the nasty surprises one gets when one wakes up in the morning to find that the market will open more than 150 points away from the prior close are predominantly associated with falls in the market. Other than the surprise election victory by John Major in 1992, I can't remember when the FTSE last opened up by more than 200 points. So much for the dangers of selling short.

As regards individual equities, the principal danger is shorting a stock that turns out to have an astonishingly good profit report, or worse yet a stock that is subject to a takeover bid. For the most part, one can avoid such stocks.

There are two perceived drawbacks to selling short. I regard one as unrealistic and the other as a virtue, not a drawback.

Perceived drawbacks to selling short

1. It is said that you can only lose 100% of your capital by going long, but you can lose more than 100% of your capital by going short (not counting the effect of leverage). The idea of losing more than 100% of your capital is hopelessly unreal. It assumes that the market or the security of which you're short will more than double without your having taken any protective or remedial action. It can happen in tiny stocks which are subject to a takeover, but you steer clear of those. You can only lose more than 100% of your capital by self-immolation. Of course if you're over-leveraged, it's less difficult to lose more than 100%, but whose fault is that?

2. Many investors buy a stock hoping for an upswing. When that hope is not realised, the stock becomes a long-term investment, which is doublespeak for their unwillingness to take a loss. Playing the market from the long side means you can fudge your errors. But because a stock might indeed rise over 100% over time, a short seller has to take his losses at some point. This is desirable. It represents discipline. You are forced to recognise your mistakes.

I suppose it is possible to swing trade from the long side only, but it would be an arrant waste of opportunity. In the United Kingdom, establishing a short position is now easy through the medium of contracts for difference (CFDs), and spread betting, which I touch on below.

Normal service

In one sense chart-based swing trading is a trend following method in that the really substantial profits are made when the market is trending up or down. But in principle there is no reason why swing trading would not be successful in a market that is in a sideways range provided that the sideways range had a significant distance between its highs and its lows, enough distance for the swing trader to make money. That was the case in early 2000. Of course when the market is in a tight trading range, it is difficult for the swing trader to make any real money. That was the case in late 2000 and the first 4 months of 2002.

It is true that for a large proportion of the time, the swing trader makes money only to give it back on the next swing trade. It would be too easy were it not so. The swing trader tries to grind out a series of small profits and losses, all the time preserving his capital, **waiting for a substantial swing or a linear phase** to unfold when a succession of winners can be put together. To my mind, if one had to draw a graph of the swing trader's capital it would not remotely resemble the straight line graph of 45° which one sometimes sees in cartoons. Instead it would resemble a staircase with a long tread. For extended periods the swing trader makes little or no money but that counts as success because he is preserving his firepower for when it really matters.

Beginners to swing trading often don't realise this point. They bemoan their lack of sustained success, and often, I suspect, try to break out of a rut by taking extra, unjustified risks. Patience is not only a virtue, but a necessity, and a difficult one to master in swing trading.

Linear phases and how to spot them

First I should explain what I mean by 'linear phase'. Go back to the chart of the FTSE in the year 2000 on page 8. You'll see 2 phases in the first 3 months of the year when prices moved broadly in a straight line. There was very little sideways movement. The angles of descent and of ascent were steep. Those were obvious linear phases. Linear phases don't always have straight line movement all the time. There may be periods when the market is rising or falling in a typical wave pattern. But linear phases involve substantial changes in price over several weeks or months, during part of which time the price movement resembles, broadly speaking, a straight line.

I am not sure it is possible to know *in advance* that a linear phase is about to happen. If it were, one could sit out the difficult phases and wait solely for the substantial swings and linear phases. But in Chapter 5, I describe various ways of improving one's chances of identifying and trading potential linear phases. It doesn't always work, but I regard the results as pretty good overall.

One thing it *is* possible to detect is when one is the middle of a linear phase. Many of these phases are connected with a theme or a crisis. So in the first 6 weeks of 2000 what was forcing the FTSE down was the wholesale dumping of old economy stocks and, in particular, banks in order that institutions could scramble into high tech. In 1997 the linear phase was connected to the melt down in Asia. In 1998 it was the Russian debt default and Long Term Capital Management.

What will happen in a linear phase is that everything will point in the same direction: The point & figure charts, the bar chart, the swing chart, the moving averages, but more than that the gradient of the incline or decline will steepen materially at some point. Countertrend rallies/dips will fall well short of the previous swing high/low. Volume will pick up as institutional swing traders and hedge funds place big bets.

It is at this point that the swing trader is justified in taking bigger risks. There is usually a suitable correction or countertrend swing which enables you to get on board the linear phase with a large position. But sometimes that doesn't happen. In the brief linear phase in March/April 2000 the FTSE soared nearly 800 points in just over 5 weeks without any real correction. There was no real bout of profit-taking, no mini-downswing which could be used to take advantage of the linear phase. It was not difficult to make a profit, but it wasn't a pleasingly large one.

It is the aim of this book to provide a method for any trader, even a novice,

a. to preserve his capital rather than to squander it

b. to increase his capital modestly during non-linear phases

c. to make a killing during linear phases

My approach

I prefer equity index futures to individual equities

I was called to the Bar by the Middle Temple in July 1987. Naturally, because I was so often in court, I could only speculate on a part-time basis. I was a full-time chartist, keeping a series of bar charts and point & figure charts, but my trading opportunities had to be tailored to my working commitments.

Moreover, I needed a method which had a mechanical component to it. That drew me to swing charts. And I needed a market which would take stop orders including OCO ('one cancels the other') orders so that orders would get executed automatically whilst I was on my feet cross-examining. At the time the US treasury bond futures market was the dominant market in the world, so that is what I started off with. Later I moved on to equity index futures and options. That was also suitable. I could go off to court without having to worry about a profit warning or any specific company risk.

I am still primarily a speculator in equity index futures and options. I prefer to avoid specific company risk, and index trading allows me to do that. When an investment bank issues a buy or sell note on a particular stock or group of stocks, it does affect the index, but not by much. But if you have a position in an individual stock, a buy or sell note, particularly one that makes startling claims or forecasts, can dramatically affect your position. The split in my speculation between equity index futures/options and individual equities is of the order of 85-15, although the individual equity side is growing slowly.

I seldom look at any stocks outside the biggest 50 or so companies, for 3 reasons:

1. When trading from the long side, there should be little solvency risk with the biggest companies. Companies like Marconi, Enron and Tyco have rather upset this notion, but I do think it holds true generally. When trading from the short side, there is little risk of a hostile takeover bid for such big companies. For trading purposes, the potential for unpleasant surprises is therefore minimised.

2. The volume of shares traded in the these stocks is the highest. This lends integrity to the price movement, and the charts of these stocks have clearer buy and sell signals and fewer false signals.

3. Swing charts (see Chapters 3, 4 and 5) work best with active stocks.

Jim Slater, famous speculator, says 'Elephants don't gallop' by which he means that the very size of the top 50 companies inhibits the extent of their likely price movement. He's right. But he is also not a chartist or a swing trader. He and many others scour the market for 'ten-baggers' - usually smallish stocks that may go up ten fold in price (which Barclays Bank is certainly not going to do in my lifetime).

It must be very gratifying, but I am not sure that I'd know a ten-bagger if I saw one. And if I thought I had found one, I'd be wondering why others, who have a good deal more time on their hands, hadn't spotted it.

I take a top down approach

Whenever I am making a decision about an individual share I am greatly influenced by how the FTSE index chart sets up. Sometimes the primacy I afford the index chart turns out to be misplaced as the particular share I am watching turns out to be independently strong or weak. I fail to capitalise because the index chart did not tell the same story. It can't be helped. I can't get used to buying a stock when my index charts suggest that the market as a whole is going down.

I'm a market timer, a top down man - I try to get the market right, then the sector and if you get those two right, it's difficult to lose money on an individual share.

I am not suggesting that this method is one that everyone should adopt. It is simply the method that I am most comfortable with. You have only to read Kevin Goldstein-Jackson's articles in the *Financial Times* to see how well it is possible to do by being a bottom up man. But he, like Jim Slater, is looking for ten-baggers.

When Berkshire Hathaway reported its profits in early May 2002, Warren Buffett was plagued by questions from investors about what calculations to make in order to buy stocks. He said, "There is no single metric I can give you…people always want a formula. It doesn't work that way".

I understand the desire for a formula. To a certain extent, charts are formulaic. It's largely a rule-based discipline. The popularity of charts is growing, exponentially I believe, precisely because investors and traders want a 'metric'.

When I do my top down analysis to determine the trend of the market as a whole, I use primarily swing charts. They are intentionally governed by rules. But rules should be there to serve you, not master you, so in some limited circumstances, I have changed rules to make matters more flexible. Also, in some respects, such as the tricky decision when to take profits, I have no magic formula (save that I like to take them early and often!).

The tooled-up swing trader

Equipment

How life changed in the late Nineties. In the Eighties, I had a set of charts which I updated manually, and access to a landline telephone to phone my broker to discover what was happening. That was the sum total of my equipment.

I still keep a few charts which I update manually. But now a financial pager gives me near real-time prices. I use Reuters mini-pager (now owned by Sila Communications). Is it any better than other pagers on the market? I don't know. But what has been important for me is the accommodating way that Reuters/Sila will arrange for me to have, for free, a mini-pager when I am in South Africa or America on holiday (I know, I know you're thinking how sad, but I've never pretended not to be an addict). It costs £86 per month inclusive of VAT for the equity service, LIFFE and Eurex. Good charting software has traditionally cost about £600-£900. End-of-day price feeds are reasonably priced, but real-time price feeds have always been expensive (over £1,000 per annum). I've always used Indexia/Updata software, and various different price feeds. Updata have recently launched a product that should revolutionise matters for private investors. The software now comes free and the live feed, arranged through S&P, costs £57 per month.

I doubt that one actually needs a financial pager. I have one only because there are times when I have no access to a computer. The internet provides various sources of cheap or free share price information (e.g. Advfn.com). Free charting software on the internet is fairly mediocre. One of the honourable exceptions is www.stockcharts.com.

Many share price quote vendors will vaunt to the skies level II information - (mainly market depth). Pay up for it if you want. It is vital for day traders and overnight traders, so they say, but you certainly do not need level II to apply the principles in this book.

Beware of manipulation of the market depth. You will see on premium bulletin boards day traders saying "Look at the ratio of sellers to buyers in Vodafone - it's 12 to 1!!". If you were a hedge fund with a short position, how would you encourage the market to go down. Place a whole lot of sell orders on the electronic order book some way above the market, thereby reinforcing the impression of a large ratio of sellers to buyers, and then remove those orders if serious buying comes in. Not very difficult.

Capital

What sort of capital is required? There is no minimum size account. Given that the spread betting firms will take almost any bet, however small, and will offer credit (against proof of liquid assets) I suppose one could start with next to nothing. However I found in my early days of commodity trading, when I put up the bare minimum, that it so restricted my trading that it was next to useless, especially for a novice, as I was. Just like W.D. Gann, I started off losing money in the way that 90% of futures traders do. In the early 1980s, new to and excited by commodity trading, I put up $5,000 and lost every penny. I saved some more from my salary. I put up another $5,000 and again lost nearly every penny. But this represented progress. The first occasion it took me 3 to 4 months to lose the $5,000. The second occasion it took 18 months. I shan't bore you with an entire life history, but having a small account puts ferocious psychological pressure on one. Each loss is a hammer blow.

How much should you risk on each trade? It's impossible to say. It depends on each individual's risk profile. Courtney Smith[2] makes a persuasive case for not over-trading. He suggests that having decided where your stop loss should be, you should not risk more than 1% of your equity on any trade. Undoubtedly it is the right advice for beginners. More experienced traders may feel able to risk more. I certainly do.

Type of account

I have the lot. A futures and options account, a CFD account and more than one spread betting account.

Contracts for difference (CFDs) are a neat way of getting round the silly stamp duty which successive British governments have insisted on imposing on the purchase of shares. They permit traders to mimic the buying and selling of individual equities, but, by an artificial device, the traders do not technically own the shares, but rather a contractual right or obligation. The economic effect is virtually the same as holding the shares or shorting the shares.

An account to trade CFDs can be opened with any of the usual stockbrokers who offer this service. In addition, a number of spread betters offer not only a spread betting facility but also a CFD facility. It is important to understand the difference. In a CFD trade, the speculator is marked to market every day and is charged interest on the full value of any long position, and is paid interest on the full value of any short position. Of course as interest rates are so low, the amount of interest which one earns is piffling, but it is noteworthy that a short position will actually earn you money whilst you are holding it. It used to be the case that CFDs were much cheaper than spreadbets, but spread betting firms have altered their products so that they are now virtually identical to CFDs. The principal difference between a CFD trade and a spread bet is that the CFD trade is fully taxable, whereas spread bets are not taxable.

The growth of the spread betting business has been a real boon to the private investor in Britain, not only because of the tax advantages, but also because of the variety of share products which can be traded. In the United States, trading sector indices is big business (through exchange traded funds or 'ETFs'), but in Britain there was no real way to trade the FTSE sector indices until spread betting came along. Some spread betting firms are open 24 hours and will hold stop losses for you, whereas the London Stock Exchange's electronic order book does not accept stop losses.

2. *New Thinking in Technical Analysis* by Rick Bensignor (Bloomberg Press 2000), Chapter 12

3 GANN SWING CHARTS

- W.D. Gann's secret

- Standard Dow theory compared to Gann

- Changes of trend and intermediate swings

- Construction of a Gann swing chart

W.D. Gann's secret

W.D. Gann may have been the greatest trader who ever lived. Here is how he described the 'secret' of his trading in an interview with *Ticker and Investment Digest* in 1909:

> "For the past 10 years I have devoted my entire time and attention to this speculative market. Like many others, I lost thousands of dollars and experienced the usual ups and downs incidental to the novice who entered the market without preparatory knowledge of the subject.
>
> I soon began to realise that all successful men, whether lawyers, doctors or scientists, devoted years of time to the study and investigation of that particular pursuit or profession before attempting to make any money out of it.
>
> Being in the brokerage business myself and handling large accounts, I had opportunities seldom afforded the ordinary man for studying the cause of success and failure in the speculation of others. I found that over 90 per cent of the traders who go into the market without knowledge or study usually lose in the end. I soon began to note the periodical recurrence of a rise and fall in stocks and commodities. This led me to conclude that natural law was the basis of market movements. I then decided to devote 10 years of my life to the study of natural law as applicable to the speculative markets and devote my best energies towards making speculation a profitable profession. After exhaustive researches and investigations of the known sciences, I discovered that the law of vibration enabled me to accurately determine the exact points at which stocks or commodities should rise and fall within a given time. It is impossible here to give an adequate idea of the law of vibrations as I apply it to the markets. However the layman may be able to grasp some of the principles when I state that the law of vibration is the fundamental law upon which wireless telegraphy, wireless telephone and phonographs are based . . .
>
> By knowing the exact vibration of each individual stock I am able to determine at what point each will receive support and what point the greatest resistance is to be met . . .
>
> From my extensive investigations, studies and applied tests, I find that not only do the various stocks vibrate, but that the driving forces controlling the stocks are also in a state of vibration."

I pause. Laws of vibration? If this sounds deranged to you, you are probably not alone. W.D. Gann placed weight on the fact that the number 7 occurs in the Bible more often than any other number, he relied on natural law and more. Hundreds of thousands of people have heard of W.D.

Gann, but I imagine that many are wary of using his techniques, insofar as they are capable of being understood, because they sound fanciful, to put it charitably.

But interestingly *Ticker and Investment Digest* appointed one of its representatives to monitor Gann's trading. The following results were achieved.

> "During the month of October 1909 in 25 market days, Mr. Gann made 286 transactions in various stocks on both the long and short side of the market. 264 of these transactions resulted in profits; 22 in losses. The capital with which he operated was doubled 10 times so that at the end of the month he made 1,000%."

Some of what Gann said may be too strange to give credit to but he made some astoundingly accurate public predictions including that of the Great Crash in 1929 and he is said to have accumulated $50 million during the first half of the 20th Century. (Sceptics point out that there appeared to be no trace of the $50 million after his death).

There are traders who are vociferously defensive of some of the more mystical aspects of Gann's work. So be it. It is not the remit of this book to bury or to praise Gann.

Although Gann angles are fairly widely used by market traders, I don't use them. The part of Gann's work that fascinates me is his swing charts. They are logically defensible and they work, although as you will see I have made some modifications. **I believe that the intelligent use of swing charts will materially enhance the profitability of your trading.**

I don't know whether Gann ever met Charles Dow but I assume he must have read Dow's editorials in the Wall Street Journal at the turn of the 19th century. Gann swing charting is a short-term variation of a part of standard Dow theory.

Standard Dow theory compared to Gann

There are several elements to standard Dow theory. But at the heart of it is an attempt to identify, from the price action, when a bull market becomes a bear market and vice versa.

A bull market by definition has higher highs and higher lows. It resembles an irregular staircase. After the market has made a swing low (point A), and it resumes its uptrend, it is a warning sign when the next upward swing fails to make new highs. See point B on the chart over the page. The price action suggests that the enthusiasm of buyers is eroding. When the subsequent downward swing breaches a previous swing low, the erosion of support from buyers is confirmed. This is a sell signal. See point C on the chart over the page.

Don't take my word for it. Look at the charts and you will see hundreds of examples of it. In Dow theory these swings would be substantial swings lasting many weeks if not months.

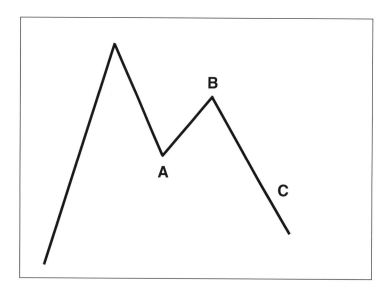

fig 3.1

But standard Dow theory did not regard it as a sell signal if, after making new highs, the subsequent downward swing breached a previous swing low, as in fig 3.2 below.

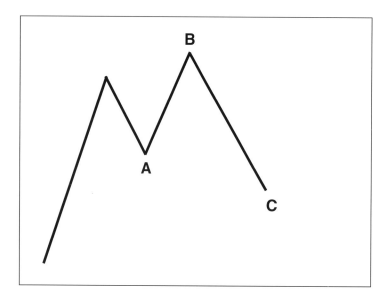

fig 3.2

There would need to be a lower high, optimally before the swing low was breached, as in the first diagram. It is in this respect that Gann swing charts differ from standard Dow theory. In Gann swing charting theory, a sell signal is generated whenever a prior swing low is breached (whether or not the last swing high was lower than the one before that). And as I've mentioned, whereas the swings in Dow theory last many weeks or months, in Gann swing charting, a valid swing low may be created by a retracement lasting *just 3 days*. You may think, at this point, that 3 days of price action can hardly be determinative of the market's trend. You are in for a surprise.

Change of trend and intermediate swings

The main use of a Gann swing chart is to identify and trade a change in trend. But Gann made it clear that the swing chart can also be used for trading the intermediate swings.

Look at the Reuters chart below, covering the period June 2000 to February 2001. It is clear that there is a broad uptrend until early September 2000, followed by a broad downtrend. Within the uptrend there are several good buying opportunities, when Reuters makes swing lows at points A, B and C. Likewise, during the downtrend, there are several good selling opportunities when Reuters makes swing highs at points D, E, F and G. It's the capture of these opportunities which inspires me.

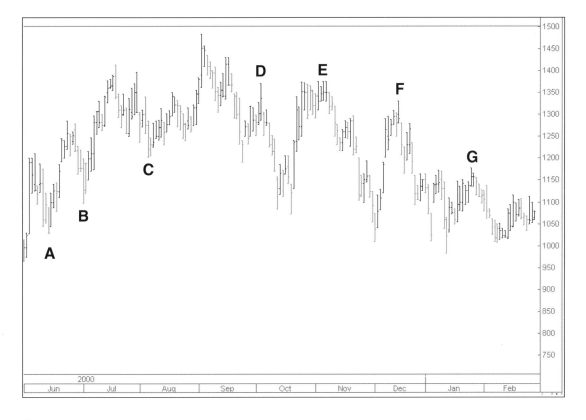

fig 3.3

What the swing chartist/swing trader attempts to do is to trade either the whole of the broad uptrend/downtrend or sections of it by trading the swing highs/lows, or both.

Construction of a Gann swing chart

I deal with this only briefly because my modifications do not actually require the swing chart to be drawn.

A swing chart is a line superimposed on a bar chart highlighting the swing highs and swing lows. As prices go up, one draws a line connecting the daily highs of the share price. Inside days (lower high, higher low) are ignored. Down days are ignored until, according to Gann, three consecutive down days occur. At that point, the line swings to the bottom of the third bar, and is connected to each lower low made by the bar chart. Again inside days are ignored, as are up days until there are three consecutive days up.

The result looks like an irregular wave pattern (fig 3.4), although it is often drawn in the form of a Manhattan chart (fig 3.5).

fig 3.4

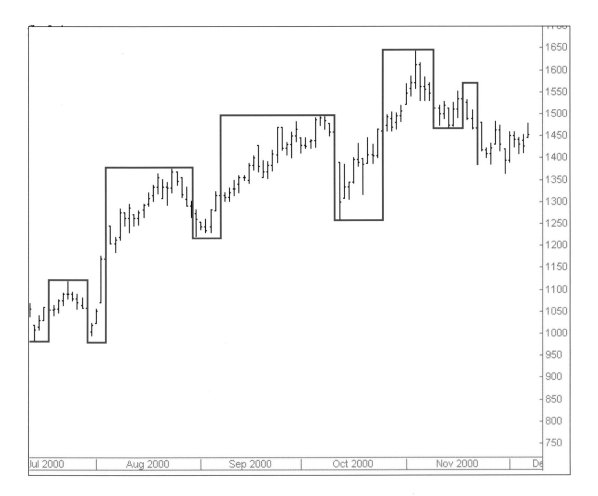

fig 3.5

That all sounds simple enough. One can get very excited when looking at the Gann swing chart. The clear pattern of rising lows makes it look as if there is easy money to be made, and indeed it does portray the short-term trend very well. However when it comes to applying the chart for trading purposes, it seems to me to have a number of serious drawbacks, so I have made a number of modifications, which I explain in detail in the next chapter.

With any swing chart, an uptrend will be characterised by successively higher swing lows and, in the main, higher swing highs. In a downtrend, there will be successively lower swing highs, and, in the main, lower swing lows. There are two central tenets of a Gann swing chart:

1. The trend changes from up to down when and only when a previous swing low formed during the uptrend is breached.

Closing prices are irrelevant. When the lowest point of the last bull market market swing low is breached on any day thereafter, it is a sell signal - a new downtrend has commenced. Vice versa for a change in trend from down to up. See point C on fig 3.1 and fig 3.2 in this chapter. I make no modification to this principle.

2. Thereafter, each time the market makes a new and lower swing high and then declines to fresh lows, the downtrend is re-affirmed, and for aggressive traders, a fresh sell signal is given.

I have modified this principle to try to capitalise earlier on the fresh sell signal.

Gann swing charts have a distinct mechanical flavour to them. Indeed Gann called his method 'The Mechanical Method & Trend Indicator'. It is a deliberate attempt to impose a rule-based system on the market. This is an excellent idea, because it leaves less room for the foibles of individual traders to intrude. But whereas some rule-based systems are weak on logic, and appear to work only because empirically they can be shown to have worked in the past, swing charts have considerable logic underpinning them. They delineate exactly where supply and demand dominated the market on previous occasions. Insofar as that is an inadequate guide to the future, it is a fault common to all charts. Moreover the swing chart fits very well the rhythm of the market which everyone can see unfolds in swings of various lengths and amplitudes.

In my opinion, provided one is dealing with high volatility stocks or equity indices, the swing chart is by far the best chart available to traders. I understand that many accomplished swing traders will already be using their own favourite chart. But most swing traders will not have tried seriously to harness the power of swing charts. I assure you it is worth the effort.

In any event, you can use swing charts in conjunction with your own favourite chart. I use two different types of chart. Since I am a top down type, and the first question I ask before making any trading decision is, 'what is the trend of the market?', it follows that my first and most important port of call is my swing chart of the market. But as you will see, swing charts on individual equities have more variable results so I use a combination of swing charts and point & figure charts and, as regards individual equities, the point & figure charts have the final say.

4 MODIFIED SWING CHARTS

- Definitions

- Faults with the Gann swing chart

- Modification 1 - 'Get in Early'

- Modification 2 - 'If the third day is an outside day, it is part of the correction'

- Modification 3 - 'Relax the requirement for three consecutive days'

- Modification 4 - 'Count trading days only'

- Buy and sell signals

- Change of trend signals

- Continuation of trend signals

- Problem areas

- Tailpiece

Definitions

As I've said, at heart I am a market timer. Timing the broad and the lesser swings of the market as a whole is what motivates me.

I never fail to look at the message conveyed by my point & figure charts, but for timing the market as a whole and for trading index futures and options, my swing charts dominate. You, the reader, could go further. It is entirely possible to time the markets, and to trade index futures and options by using swing charts only. If you don't like point & figure, so be it. The swing chart is a winner all by itself.

The modifications I have made to Gann's swing charting theory represent my attempt to make the swing charts as effective as possible from a trader's perspective and to enhance my timing of the market.

As I've mentioned, my modifications mean that you don't actually have to draw a swing chart. Interpretation and trading can be done from an ordinary bar chart.

It is the highs and lows recorded by the bar chart which are important. In this chapter, when I refer to an 'up day' I mean a day with a higher high and a higher low than the previous day. The closing price is not relevant to this definition, although of course in general terms the close is an important tool from which useful inferences may be drawn. Likewise a 'down day' is a day with a lower high and a lower low. Inside days (lower high, higher low) are generally ignored. Outside days (higher high, lower low), which do represent significant price action, receive variable treatment (explained in the glossary).

Faults with the Gann swing chart

The principal focus of a Gann swing chart, and of my modified swing charts, is the identification of *relevant* countertrend rallies/dips. They form a reference point both for trading and for determining the trend.

Gann regarded a one day rally in a downtrend as irrelevant, however substantial the rally. What his method seeks to do is to focus on those corrections in a short-term trend which portray an important level where supply exceeded demand or vice versa. The problem is how to define the important, and exclude the unimportant in a way which allows for as little subjective opinion as possible.

In a downtrend, the standard Gann swing chart turns up and registers a countertrend rally, a swing high, only when there are 3 *consecutive* days of higher highs. I regard that as a bit of a fault. But much, much worse is the notion that the countertrend rally is over and the main downtrend has resumed only when there are a further 3 consecutive days down. The standard Gann chart gives one a very good idea of direction, but the stipulation that the main downtrend has resumed only if there are 3 consecutive days down is not only unwieldy for traders, it is counterintuitive.

It is obvious, on a glance at the past history of any chart in a downtrend (uptrend), that the main trend has resumed as soon as the countertrend rally (dip), the correction, is over.

Of course, the tricky bit is to determine in real time exactly when that has happened. I do not believe that task is aided by the inflexible requirement that the main trend resumes only when there are 3 consecutive down days after the countertrend rally. Take for example the FTSE in May 1999.

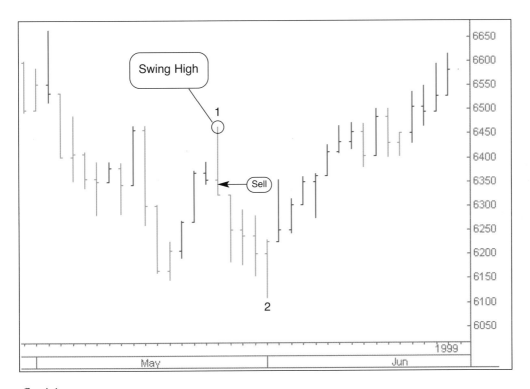

fig 4.1

1.   The market made a swing high on 24th May. It is obvious (with hindsight) from the chart that the correction, the countertrend rally, ended after the high was made that day, but -

2.   The standard Gann swing chart would signal that the main trend had resumed only on the third day down, by which time most of the move was already over, and it would give a (repeat) sell signal only on the breach of the previous swing low which happened on the fourth day down, the 28th May which was the very day the downswing ended.

My modifications mean that you would be able to act as if the main trend had resumed on the exact day that it did in fact resume, the 24th May.

Shortly before he died, Gann wrote in longhand, across his typed notes about trading grains, that a 2 day swing chart was more useful. Whether he meant that generally or in respect of grains only is not clear. In other words, instead of insisting on 3 consecutive days down (or up), Gann was apparently suggesting that 2 consecutive days were sufficient. But even a 2 day swing chart would have turned down only on 26th May, by which time the market had fallen substantially from its actual swing high.

A further huge drawback of Gann's swing chart theory is the notion that a repeat sell signal is given only when the last swing low is breached. Of course, breaching the previous swing low is indeed important confirmation that the downtrend is continuing, and if it were practical to wait that long before selling short in a downtrend or buying in an uptrend, I would be delighted to do so. But the stop loss involved would be crippling (at any rate for a trader with my risk profile).

Look at fig 4.1 above. Standard Gann practice (when pyramiding, as he called trading the intermediate swings) is to sell short at 6146 when the swing low is breached and place the stop loss above the swing high established on 24th May, namely at 6463. That's a stop loss of 317 points.

Even if one bent the rules slightly and sold short on the day that the standard Gann swing chart signalled a resumption of the main trend, the stop loss required would be so large as to make the risk/reward ratio hopelessly unattractive. A standard 3 day swing chart would have turned down on 27th May, so the stop loss required would be 263 points if you sold on the close. A standard 2 day swing chart would have turned down the day before but the stop loss required would be still be 227 points. These stop losses would be ruinous. As you will see in due course, the profit from each successful intermediate swing trade in the FTSE typically falls in the bracket of 150-400 points, although profits are occasionally larger, particularly in linear phases.

I wouldn't dream of risking over 200 points on a FTSE trade. Sometimes I forgo a trade if the potential stop loss is too large. There can't be more than a couple of occasions in my life when I've risked over 150 points on a FTSE trade.

Using my modifications a short position would have been established on 24th May at 6344, an improvement of 144 points (at least) on the 3 day swing chart and 107 points on the 2 day chart. Whilst I'd prefer my stop loss in FTSE to be under 100 points, that is not always possible. With my modifications, the stop loss here would have been 119 points which is high-ish but acceptable.

Even without pyramiding (trading the intermediate swings), you will find that the standard Gann swing chart looks superb and is occasionally superb to trade, but often produces steep losses, which negate much of the worth of the chart. That's why I've made modifications. Not everyone will agree with my modifications to Gann swing chart theory, but here they are.

Modification 1 – 'Get in Early'

Like Gann, I look for a 3+ day movement to identify a countertrend swing, **but I trade with the trend on the first day after the countertrend swing appears to end**. In short, I use a 3 day swing chart to set up the trade and a 1 day swing chart to activate the trade. One could call it a 3 bar/1bar swing chart. Effectively I am assuming that after the market has a 3+ day rally in a bear market (or a 3 day decline in a bull market), the first day that the market reverts to trend means that a swing high (low) has been established. This may sound complicated, but it is not. It is simplicity itself. It is merely complicated to describe. Look at the FTSE chart for 8th March 2001.

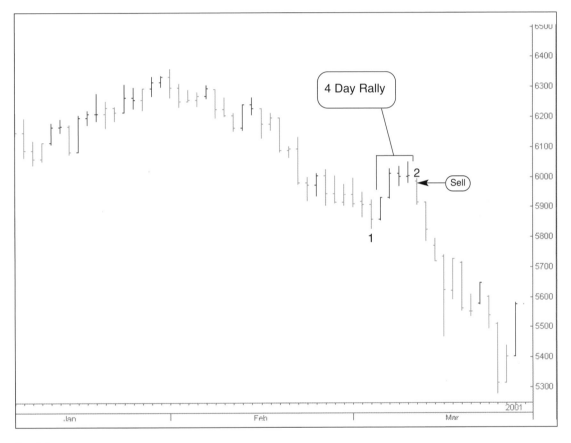

fig 4.2

The market was plainly in a downtrend, having crashed in February through the January lows. The swing trader is looking for a countertrend rally to add to a short position or to initiate one.

1.	The decline ends on 2nd March and there is a 3 day rally on 5th, 6th and 7th March. From 7th March onwards, I am looking to sell the market on the first breach of a previous day's low i.e. I'm looking for the first down day after a countertrend rally of at least 3 days. On 8th March I place a stop sell order underneath the lows of 7th March. But nothing happens, because on 8th March, the market makes a higher high and a higher low. It is the fourth up day of this countertrend rally.

2.	On 9th March, again I place a stop sell order this time below the lows of 8th March, and later in the day on 9th March, the previous day's low at 5981 is breached and my stop sell order is triggered. I am now short. I place a protective stop loss above the assumed swing high (the high of 8th March) at 6051.

It works perfectly. The market falls 500 points in 4 days. Have I chosen a good example to impress you? Of course! But I won't be shirking the trickier situations. I'll deal with them as I go along.

Once again a 2 day and 3 day standard Gann chart would have got one short, this time successfully, at much worse levels, and the size of the potential stop loss would have been a big deterrent.

Modification 2 - 'If the third day is an outside day, it is part of the correction'

This modification deals with outside days. Please see the glossary for a fuller treatment of outside days. At this point, I am dealing with how to treat the third (and potentially crucial) day in a countertrend rally if it doesn't have a nice, simple higher high and higher low. What happens if it has a higher high but a lower low? Does that count as part of the rally or not?

> • If the market has a 2 day rally and on the third day it makes a higher high, I regard that as an upturn in the swing chart, even if it later makes a lower low on that third day. Many swing chartists follow this principle, but not all do so which is why I've classified it as a modification.

> • As soon as the market has made the higher high on the third day, I place a stop order to sell below the low of the second day.

Look at fig 4.3, the FTSE chart for 28th January 2000.

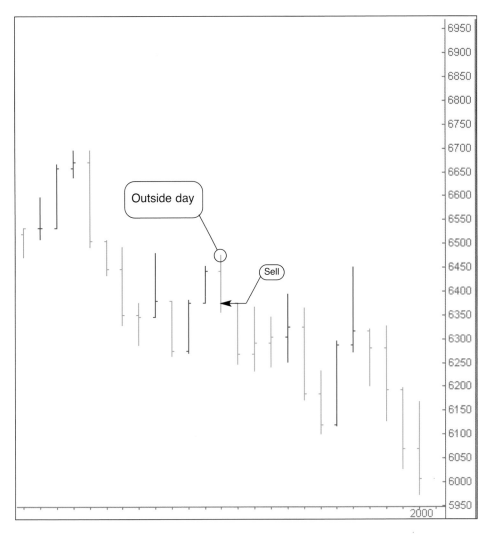

fig 4.3

The market rallied on 26th and 27th January and opened up on 28th January making a third consecutive higher high. Place a stop sell order below the low of 27th March, and later on 28th March, the stop is hit and a short position is established. This is not too large a modification. Effectively one is trading an outside day which in standard bar charting terms is indeed regarded as bearish. This modification also explains the short position established on 24th May 1999 in the first chart in this chapter.

Naturally the same principles hold true in an uptrend, when the third day of a countertrend dip is an outside day, and the market, having first moved lower, later takes out the highs of the previous day.

Modification 3 – 'Relax the requirement for three consecutive days'

If you wait for a perfect 3 consecutive days up or down, you may end up feeling a bit like Vladimir and Estragon[3]. What was Gann trying to say when he insisted on 3 consecutive days up? It seems to me one can fairly conclude that Gann was saying that a one day rally, however strong, is unimportant. The same is true of two consecutive days up or down (although late in life, Gann apparently recanted, at least in part, on this point).

But you will often find that the market is not quite so accommodating as to go up and down in consecutive three day spans. Can it really have been that important for the swing chart to turn up only when the up days are consecutive? It seems to me that this is the over-rigid application of mechanical rules. Surely Gann was saying that to be significant, a corrective rally or a dip had to last at least three days. If the market goes down on two consecutive days and then up on the third day but then falls again on the fourth day, that seems to me to be a valid swing low in the making.

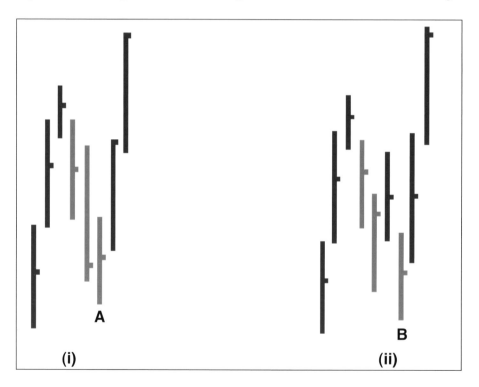

fig 4.4

Look at (i) and (ii). Assume the trend is up. The standard 3 day countertrend pullback is shown in (i). A swing low is established at point A. According to Gann, point B in (ii) does not qualify as a swing low, because the down days are not consecutive. I suggest there is no substantive difference between (i) and (ii) when it comes to defining a swing low. And it is important to be clear about what is and what is not a swing low, because it represents the trend change point. So in (i) and (ii) above, if the market should later fall through points A and B, Gann would see a change in trend in (i) but no change in trend in (ii). That cannot be right. Look at the FTSE chart for August 1998:

fig 4.5

1.   A low is made on 12th August 1998 at 5350.

2.   The next day Friday 13th August is an up day.

3.   The 16th is a down day because both the high and low (at 5398, 2 points lower than the previous low of 5400) are lower than on the 13th.

4.   The next 2 days are up days. It seems to me that a valid swing high has been created.

You don't need a rule that the up/down days have to be consecutive. It meets the heart of the principle employed in swing charting to permit more haphazard rallies to be counted as part of a swing high. I don't regard a one day interruption to the span of up days or down days as significant. That is easy to apply. The situation is more tricky when more than one day interrupts the countertrend 3 day rally/dip.

Complex swing highs and lows

Look at any bar chart and you will see that sometimes the swing high or low is a rather complex affair. What I look for is a total of 3 days up or down, whether or not they are consecutive, provided they occur in a relatively short space of time. In other words I disregard the fact that there may have been even 2 days or more interrupting the correction. Look at the chart for Barclays in October 2001.

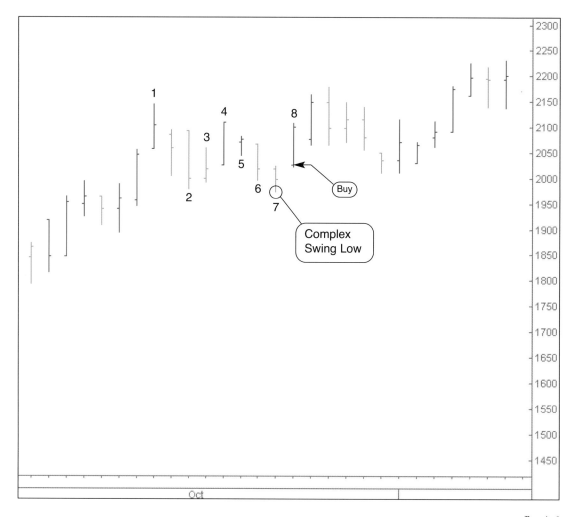

fig 4.6

1. Barclays makes a high of 2144p on 11th October.

2. The next 2 days (12th and 15th October) are down days.

3. 16th October is an inside day. Ignore.

4. 17th October is an up day. Perhaps Barclays is not going to make a swing low at this point.

5. 18th October is an inside day. Ignore. Already 5 days have elapsed since the swing high, but I regard only 2 of them as relevant. I haven't yet given up hope that this market may be in the course of forming a relevant swing low.

6. 19th October is a down day.

7. Monday 22nd October is also a down day, helpfully with a low below the low of 15th October. I am also encouraged by the fact that the range for the day i.e. the difference between the high and the low is narrow, suggesting no real selling pressure.

8. 23rd October, buy when Barclays breaches the high of 22nd October (2023p). Place a stop loss below the low of 22nd October (1974p), on the assumption that that point represents the swing low.

The assumption is borne out as 1974p is not breached and Barclays trades up to over 2300p by early January.

Note that the up day on 17th October must not exceed the swing high of 2144p. If it does, a new swing high will have been created and I will wait for a new 3 day retracement.

Deciding whether or not the low of 22nd October should be characterised as a swing low is no mere academic debate. The whole basis of trading with swing charts depends upon identifying swing lows (or highs), the later breach of which is regarded as significant. So for example in the above case of Barclays, if the price had fallen after 24th October, my modification would mean that a stop loss would be activated at 1974p, *and crucially that the trend would be regarded as having changed from up to down at that point*. A short position could then be established at that point. The standard Gann swing chart would not call a change in trend even if Barclays went down as low as 1500p (because no consecutive 3 day swing low had been breached). Look at the above chart. How is it sensible to regard Barclays as still in an uptrend if it had fallen after 24th October to the 1500p level?

Purists will say that the identification of this kind of complex swing low is no longer entirely mechanical. An element of judgment has crept in. I agree. I think the swing chart is all the better for this modification. Mechanical rules need to yield to common sense sometimes.

An example of a share *not* making a complex swing high is Marconi in January 2001.

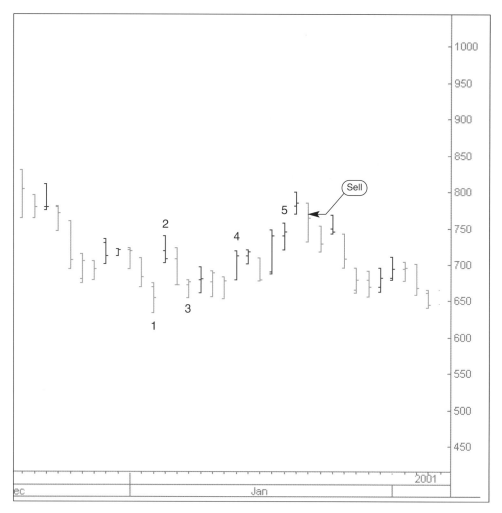

fig 4.7

1. On 3rd January Marconi makes a low at 634p in the course of its downtrend. That evening Mr Greenspan makes a surprisingly aggressive inter-meeting cut in interest rates, which

2. produces a prodigious rally the next day as Marconi touches 740p.

3. The next 5 trading days are messy. There are 2 down days followed by one up day followed by 2 down days. I don't draw any firm conclusions, but so far this doesn't look much like a swing high in the course of forming.

4. 12th and 13th January are up days.

Note: I do not count this as a 3 day rally for 2 reasons. First, there are a lot of days between the first up day and the third day. This is not conclusive, but I am not convinced this is all part of the same rally. It may be, but why take the risk? Secondly, and more importantly, the putative swing high on 13th January is well below the high of the first up day (4th January).

If I sell short which of the two is the swing high? Where do I place my stop loss? Too many imponderables. Don't touch this stock when it trades lower on 16th January.

5.   On 17th January 2001 Marconi storms higher, exceeding the 4th January high of 740p. Now there is a decent 3 day rally, and one can prepare to go short. A prior day's low is breached on 22nd January and a short position can be established below 769p. Marconi never sees this level again and never will.

At this point in the book, we are looking at matters only from the perspective of swing charts. In fact, as I've already pointed out, I also use point & figure charts. I did not short and would not have shorted Marconi on 22nd January 2001 (more's the pity!) because the point & figure chart had taken on an attractive aspect. I would have been in two minds what to do, and I would therefore have chosen something easier.

Combinations

An example of a complex swing high combined with an outside day was provided in January 2000. The much-hyped Y2K fears turned out to be largely groundless. In the first 3 trading days of the year the market crashed through the swing lows made in December and so one was looking for an opportunity to add to or to initiate a short position.

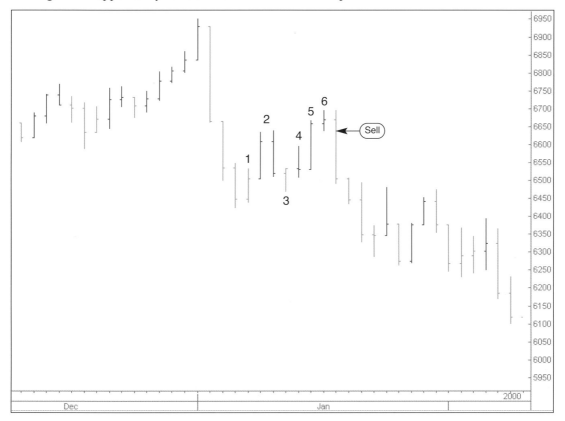

fig 4.8

The low is made on 6th January.

1.   7th January is an inside day. Ignore.

2.   10th January and 11th January are up days.

3.   12th January is a down day.

4.   13th January is an up day but its high is well short of the high of the second up day, so I'm not ready to sell. Optimally the high on the third day should be higher than the day you are counting as the second up day, but if it is nearly the same, I will count it as the third day up because I will have a clear place to put a stop loss.

5.   The 14th January makes a new high for the rally. Now I'm ready to sell on the first breach of a prior day's low, on the assumption that the high already made will turn out to be the swing high.

6.   In fact, the market completes another up day on 17th January, so even a standard Gann swing chart would have turned up at this point. The narrow daily range encourages me. It is suggestive of no real buying pressure. On 18th January my stop sell order is below the low of the 17th at 6637. The market trades up initially, and then collapses, triggering my stop sell order on an outside day.

Note once again that my modification means that the short position is established early. Compare a 2 bar swing chart and you see that it would have turned down only on the 19th, and a sell signal on a 2 day or 3 day swing chart would have happened only on a breach of the lows of 6th January at 6423, requiring one to risk 273 points by placing a stop loss above the 18th January highs at 6696.

It is impossible to list here all of the possible variations which a bar chart might throw up to determine whether a market has made or is still making a complex swing low or high. In essence I am trying to import the spirit of some of the mechanical rules applied by Gann, whilst still leaving open the use of some judgment. *If you're not sure whether the market has made a swing low/high, back off. Wait for it to prove it to your satisfaction.* If that means missing a good trade, so be it. There are many good trades waiting for you in the future.

Modification 4 - 'Count trading days only'

Some people who use Gann swing charts count Saturday and Sunday as a part of Friday's trading. It follows that every time there is a one day countertrend move on a Friday, the 3 day swing chart turns up or down. I fail to see the sense in this. I could be persuaded that Friday ought to carry more weight than any other day of the week, but not 3 times the weight. I count only trading days, not weekends.

Final Thoughts on my Gann modifications

There is an obvious tension between the reliability of a signal, and the desire to establish a position early so that the risk/reward ratio is favourable. As will be seen, my modifications do have some disadvantages but the balance I have struck suits my risk profile, and, I suggest, the risk profile of most swing traders.

Buy and sell signals

There are two types of buy/sell signal given by the swing chart. The first is a **change of trend signal**, and the second is a **continuation of trend signal** after a countertrend rally/dip has ended. Gann was interested primarily in change of trend signals, but you miss too much if you ignore the continuation of trend signals.

Change of trend signals

Whenever a security which has been in an uptrend, falls and breaches a previous swing low, there is a deemed change of trend. A new downtrend is established. A change to a new uptrend occurs whenever a market, which has been in a downtrend, rallies above a previous swing high. Consider the chart for HSBC in late 2000/early 2001.

fig 4.9

After a series of higher swing lows at 926p on 30th November 2000 (point A), at 934p on 15th December 2000 (point B) and at 971p at 11 January 2001 (point C) and finally at 1033p on 5th February 2001 (point D), HSBC staggers upwards to 1075p, but cannot attain the levels of the January swing highs. Twelve trading days later, it crashes through the swing low of 5th February 2001. That is the signal that the trend has changed from up to down. A short position should be established when 1033p is breached.

Note how the lower high at 1075 (point E), followed by the lower low of 5th February is a classic microcosm of Dow theory.

• At the swing low of 1033p (point D), the market consensus was that prices were cheap. From that point onwards, buyers dominated sellers, driving prices up. When that same low at 1033p was breached 12 days later, it is an obvious inference that the market consensus had altered. What was formerly considered too cheap at that level had become too expensive as sellers dominated buyers.

I hear the sceptics say suppose the market just bobs a little way below the first swing low and storms upwards again. Well that does happen sometimes. But as I've already pointed out, the chartist knows that market price action evolves over time. He assumes that there is probably a good reason for the breach of the previous swing low, and that it will take time for a new consensus to emerge. That assumption is often borne out, but plainly not invariably so.

• How far below 1033p should the short position be opened? Gann's view was that a breach by a single tick was enough, although the tick size when he was trading was eighths of a dollar. Modern Gann chartists adhere to the belief that a breach by a single tick is sufficient to constitute a buy/sell signal. I do follow this as regards indices. I tend to place my stop either 1 or 2 ticks above/below the swing high/low when trading equity indices. You may think that a single tick may not be that important, but it has the value of certainty.

Sometimes one gets caught by a false signal but I've never found it possible to place my stop-buy or stop-sell order at just the right level to avoid a false signal. Some false signals trade 2 or 3 ticks through the key level, some trade 5 to 10 ticks through, and some 20 or more. When I traded Treasury Bonds I used a stop 3 ticks away, because that did seem to avoid a number of occasions when the market traded through a previous high by 1 or 2 ticks without the breach having any enduring significance.

As regards individual equities, it is much trickier. The electronic order book does not accept stop orders; there are rogue orders at the beginning of the day, and it frequently happens that a large sell or buy order is badly handled by a broker/dealer (by hitting every bid or taking every offer in sight without regard to the real, unstated depth of the market) which distorts the market temporarily.

As a result, I do leave some margin for slippage when trading individual equities. It is often as much as 0.5%, and I suspect with illiquid stocks (which I do not trade), an even larger cushion might well be appropriate. So for example with the short sale of HSBC, I would have entered the position only when the swing low was breached by 5p i.e at 1028p. A sensible idea is to back test a security which you want to trade. Does it give many false signals and, if so, is there a certain point at which one might place a stop loss in order to avoid a reasonable percentage of the false signals?

• Stop losses. The lower high made by HSBC (point E) also provided a convenient place to put a stop loss against the short position established at 1028p. The bearish conclusion that one had drawn when HSBC made a lower high at 1075p and then crashed through 1033p would be invalidated if thereafter the share price reversed and rose above that selfsame lower swing high. The stop loss should be placed at 1080p. That represents a stop loss of 5%, which I consider to be very high - the outer limit of what is acceptable. My normal stop loss on the FTSE and the Dow is 2 - 2.5% at most; on individual equities it is around 3.5 - 4%.

• *Note* that in HSBC's case 12 trading days elapsed between the swing low of 5th February (point D) and the collapse through those swing lows. That made it relatively clear that the 5th February was a swing low, and that the days following it constituted an attempt to resume the main trend, an uptrend. They were not a continuing attempt to form a swing low. We will see in due course situations which are not so clear.

• These change of trend signals occur relatively frequently (about 4 to 9 times a year). But the swing chartist does not actually believe that each and every time a swing low or high is breached, there is a major new bull or bear market underway.

The swing chartist knows that a percentage of the 'change of trend' signals will be false, a percentage will result in an embryonic new trend about which the market has second thoughts, before reversing, leaving the swing trader with a small profit or none at all, and a percentage will result in a substantial money-making opportunity.

For example, in 1999 the FTSE gave 8 change of trend signals, of which 3 were false and 2 led nowhere (gain of only 100-150pts) before reversing. In 2000, there were 10 change of trend signals of which 1 was false and 1 led nowhere. In 2001, there were 7 change of trend signals of which 2 were false. If these numbers make unhappy reading, worry not. It all works out in the end.

Continuation of trend signals

Look at all the charts (except of course the HSBC chart) in this chapter hitherto. They all portray continuation of trend signals.

Once a change of trend has been signalled when the market breaches a previous swing high or low, the swing trader should be watching and waiting for a countertrend swing which lasts a minimum of 3 days.

I attempt to use market corrections to buy low and sell high. Naturally, I want to sell as high and buy as low as it is possible to do without taking an undue risk. Once there is a 3+ day rally in a downtrend (or a 3+ day dip in an uptrend), I am eager to identify as early as possible the ending of the correction. I assume that the first sign that the rally (dip) has failed means that the market is ready to resume the main trend.

What is the first sign of failure of a rally? I regard it as a sign of failure when the market breaches the low of the previous day.

So as soon as there has been a 3 day rally in a downtrend, I place a stop sell order below the low of the previous day. The sell order may be placed *during* the third day (see page 36 on outside days), or before the market opens on the fourth day (if there have been 3 consecutive days up) or before the market opens on the fifth, sixth, seventh or eighth day (because the market may have made a complex swing high, during the course of which a number of inside days and down days may have intervened). If this is unclear please re-read the section on complex swing highs and lows. Each day that the rally fails to break down, I move my stop sell order up to just below the low of the previous day.

The ideology underlying the continuation of trend signal is clear. During a downtrend, sellers are dominating buyers by definition. So it is significant when buyers muster enough buying power to reverse that domination. It is even more significant when that reversal proves temporary. Vice versa for uptrends.

Problem areas

There are 2 main problem areas: false starts and false signals. False starts occur only with continuation of trend signals. False signals occur mainly with change of trend signals.

False starts

In each of the above examples, the swing trader assumes that the first up day (or down day) after a simple or complex 3+ day countertrend move means that the swing low (or swing high) has been established. In each of the above examples that assumption was borne out, and the main trend did resume. But occasionally, that first up day (or down day) turns out to be a false start and the market continues to rally (fall) the very next day. It is plain that the assumption that the swing low or high was already in place has proved incorrect. That doesn't mean that the main trend will not resume. It usually means that its resumption has been postponed. Look at the chart for BSkyB in February 2000.

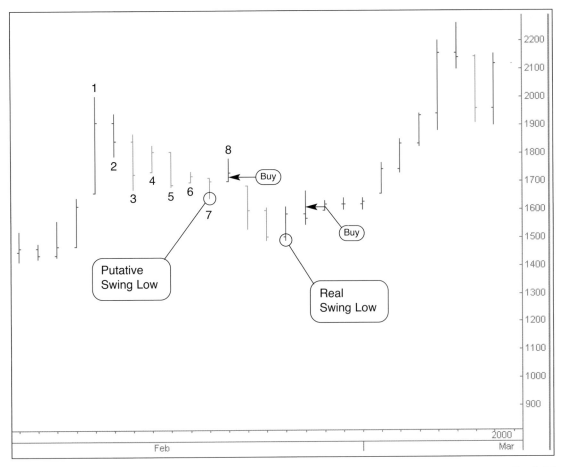

fig 4.10

1. A high is made on 9th February after a steep run at the height of the dot.com mania and it is plain that this stock needs a breather.

2. 10th February is an inside day. Ignore.

3. 11th February is a down day.

4. 14th February is an inside day. Ignore.

5. 15th February is a down day.

6. 16th February is an inside day. Ignore.

7. 17th February is a down day.

8. 18th February appears to be a buy signal after a putative swing low the previous day. The breather has ended.

49

But it's a false start. There are 2 more down days after which the swing low is in place and the main uptrend resumes.

• The sole question is whether to hang on upon the continued assumption that the swing low will be made shortly, or to take a loss and wait for the swing low to prove itself. I follow the latter course on 99% of occasions. The result is that a few times a year, I take what appears to be a needless loss. But I prefer the swing low to prove itself rather to hang on merely in the hope that the market will stabilise.

• These false starts are the biggest disadvantage of my 3bar/1bar style of trading. A standard 2 day or 3 day swing chart would not have generated a buy signal on 18th February and therefore no loss would have to be taken. But I have considered this disadvantage and I find that in the securities which I trade, the advantage of getting in early, and having a reasonable stop loss, outweighs the irritating disadvantage of these false starts.

In 1999, the FTSE produced 4 false start signals out of a total of 17 continuation of trend signals, in 2000 it was 2 false starts out of 16 and in 2001, 1 false start out of 13.

• I have read of an alternative way of deciding that the correction is over and the main trend is about to resume. Instead of placing a stop buy or sell order just above the high or low of the previous day, one could place one's buy or sell order at a point which represents a pre-defined % from the swing low or high. Such a method would have much in common with Kagi charting (although those charts work off the closing price only). In other words, one goes long or sells short if and only if the market moves more than, say 3% from the swing low. That would not have prevented the false start in the above case of BSkyB and I don't know how efficient it would be. I've never tested it. I'm perfectly happy with my method.

• **False starts are much more common in individual equities especially when not much is happening. Individual equities often take longer than market indices to form swing lows/highs.**

As a matter of impression, false starts in individual equities appear to reduce as the gradient of an ascent or descent steepens. There is a trading strategy to minimize the effect of false starts in individual equities: Trade an individual equity with call or put options. In the above example of BSkyB, on 18th February, buy a call option outright or a bull spread. That way your potential loss is fixed. When BSkyB continues making its swing low on 21st and 22nd February there is no need to stop yourself out. You hold on in the belief that the swing low will soon be formed and so it proves. If your belief is not borne out, your loss is fixed anyway.

False starts and equivocal change of trend signals

Since this topic is the trickiest part of my modified swing charts some recapitulation is warranted.

I have dealt with the typical patterns described by a market when it is making a countertrend swing low i.e a correction in an uptrend. They are:

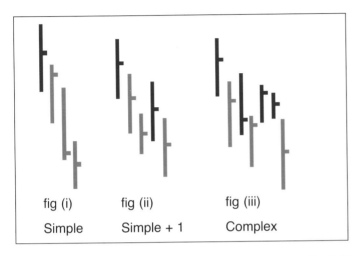

fig 4.11

Over three quarters of swing lows are formed by a simple or simple +1 swing low. In a simple +1 swing low, on one of the days before the third down day, the market moves upwards in the direction of the main trend. In a complex swing low there may be 2 or more such days, but they are not difficult to deal with because they all occur before the third day down. Until a third red bar appears there is no possibility of confusion.

The typical false start occurs the very day after the market appears to have given a buy signal. I superimpose a false start on the above diagrams.

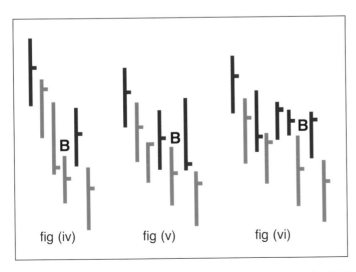

fig 4.12

In each case the buy signal was a false start as the market continued its downward correction the next day. In fig iv it looks as if the market may now make an extended simple +1 swing low. In figs. v and vi it looks as if the market is making increasingly complex swing lows.

The right thing to do would be to liquidate your long position as the market breaches the putative swing low, and wait until it forms a new swing low. Frustratingly that often happens the very next day i.e. in figs iv, v and vi above, the next bars are all blue as the market rockets upwards, which means that the loss you took on the false start was unnecessary. But occasionally the swing low doesn't happen for several days, or worse, it doesn't happen at all - the market continues falling until it gives a change of trend signal much lower down. I'd rather take the needless loss than suffer the agony of hoping that a falling market will soon form a swing low. In swing trading, hoping is a sign of error.

I added one blue bar (the putative buy signal which was in fact a false start) and one red bar (the new and real swing low) to figs i,ii and iii in order to create figs iv,v and vi. Even if I had added 2 blue bars, it seems to me that a subsequent breach of the swing low probably means that the market is continuing its correction, continuing to form a swing low, rather than changing trend. That would be a 2 day false start. But if I add 10 bars after the buy signal, during which time the putative swing low (the red bar before the false start buy signal) is not breached, it is reasonable to assume;

> a. that a valid swing low was made by that red bar.

> b. the price action since then (the 10 blue bars) is a struggling attempt to resume the main trend rather than an attempt to make a complex swing low.

> c. when the market crashes through the swing low on the 11th day after the buy signal (the 12th day after the swing low), it is not trying to make a complex swing low. It is changing its trend.

Why I have chosen an extra 10 bars? Because that it is exactly what happened in the case of HSBC on page 45.

So there are no problems differentiating a 1 or 2 day false start from a change of trend. Likewise it is not sensible to suppose that a market is producing a 10 day false start. The 11 days that the market spends above the swing low validates the swing low as an important point of support, a breach of which will be significant.

But where does one draw the line? 3 days? 4 days? 5 days? As I point out below, I assume that if a market has spent at least 3 days above its swing low, and then crashes through it, it is not a 3 day false start, it is a change of trend. Sometimes, the decision is really very easy. Look at the Dow in April 1997.

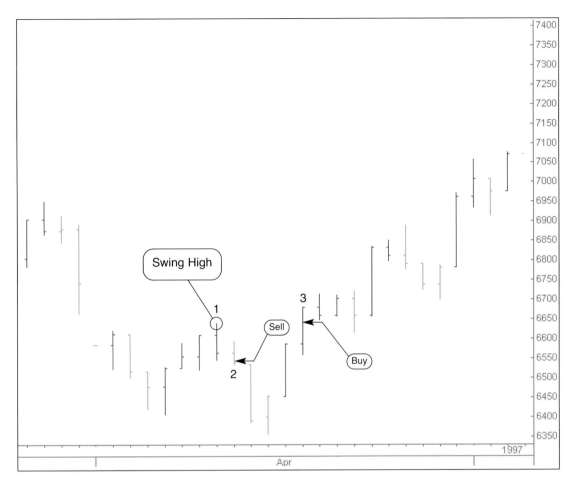

fig4.13

1.   The swing high occurs on 8th April.

2.   The sell signal occurs the next day, 9th April.

3.   Just 4 days after the continuation of trend sell signal, the market sweeps upwards breaching the high of 8th April.

The fact that the market fell to new lows validates the high of 8th April as a relevant swing high. When, on 15th April, the market breaches that swing high it cannot be a false start, a delayed complex swing high. It must be a change in trend.

But what about the Dow in October 2001?

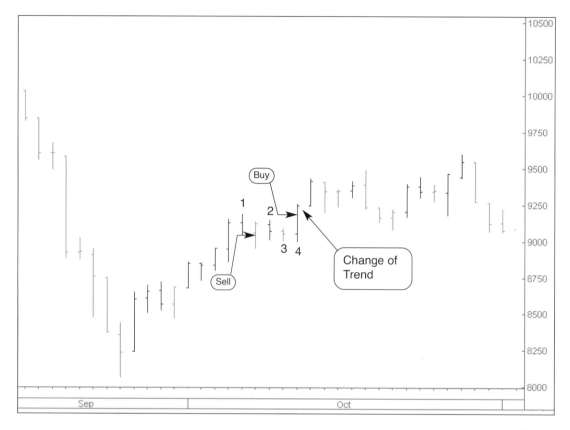

fig4.14

1. On 3rd October the Dow makes a swing high, and the next day (4th October) it generates a continuation of trend sell signal when the low of 3rd October is breached.

2. 5th October is an up day.

3. 8th October is a down day.

4. On 9th October the market soars through the highs of 3rd October. Put your hand over all the bars to the right of 9th October. Would you call this a complex swing high in the making or a change of trend? The sell signal on 4th October could be a false start, couldn't it? On the web site I wrote for at the time, I called this a change in trend. I was influenced by the following facts:

    a. There is a clear although variable relationship between time and price. The swing high from the 20th September lows to 3rd October had already taken 9 days to form. It is rare for a countertrend rally, a correction, in an index to last that long. If the rally of 9th October was all part of the same countertrend swing high, it would suggest that the swing high had taken 13 days to form which is even more rare. The length of the time and the extent of the rally were more suggestive of a change in short-term trend than a continuing correction.

b. Although it is difficult to see on the chart, the lows of 9th October were slightly below those of 8th October which means 9th October was a bullish outside day when it exceeded the highs of 8th October.

c. The minor Dow point & figure chart (25pt box) gave a buy signal on 9th October and the NASDAQ Comp main point & figure chart (20pt box) had already given one of my favourite buy signals on 3rd October.

• **My general rule of thumb is that if the market spends at least 3 days below the swing high before breaching it, it is a change of trend buy signal whereas if it spends 1 or 2 days below the swing high it is more likely to be a false start/the making of a complex swing high (and vice versa for swing lows). This rule of thumb works well on equity indices.**

It is only a rule of thumb. It is precisely because these equivocal presentations may occur that most technical analysts, including me, do not look only at one type of chart. When something equivocal does turn up, I look at my point & figure charts and the charts of other equity markets.

•. As regards individual equities, I am more strict. Individual equities often take quite some time to make a complex swing high or low, and I am reluctant to assume too readily that a change of trend has occurred. If I am in doubt, I switch to another equity.

Failed and false signals

I distinguish between failed and false signals. From time to time one gets failed signals. The chartist's assumption that there was a new consensus which would take time to develop has failed.

Failed signals are a statistical certainty. They occur both with change of trend signals and continuation of trend signals.

With a change of trend failed signal, typical market action is that the market does breach a swing high or low and moves in the desired direction, but only hesitantly and after two or three days of languishing at a level where one's profits are miniscule, it reverses and forces one to operate a stop loss.

In a continuation of trend signal, the failed signal usually takes longer than 2 or 3 days to resolve. Once again the market moves in the desired direction but without any convincing follow through. The chart of HSBC on page 45 shows a continuation of trend buy signal after the swing low at point D. That signal ultimately failed after 12 days, and the trend changed to a downtrend. In the FTSE index, I define a failed signal as one that has not moved 100 points in my favour i.e. about 1.7 - 2%.

There seems no point in displaying charts of these occasions. I have not found that they have anything particular in common which would be instructive.

In addition to the false starts described above and the spring trap reversals described below, in 1999 the FTSE had 2 failed signals out of a total of 25 signals, in 2000 5 failed signals out of a total of 26, and in 2001 3 failed signals out of a total of 20 signals.

Whereas a failed signal 'works' for a few days, without generating any worthwhile profit, before the market has second thoughts, any signal that effectively does not work at all is a false signal. Here are the notable ones:

Intraday reversals

The market advances through a swing high suggesting a change a trend. In fact, later the same day it reverses, which makes it look very much like a swing high is being completed rather than a change in trend. So the breach of the old swing high was a false buy signal. The close should be very weak to confirm this as an intraday reversal. Look at the chart opposite which shows BT in September 1998.

1.   On 15th September a 3 day rally creates a swing high at 595p.

2.   By 22nd September another 2 day rally has taken BT all the way back to a high of 595p.

3.   On 23rd September, BT opens at 589p but powers through the swing high of 595p, indicating a change in trend. Allowing for 0.5% slippage, you might place a stop buy order at 598p. The stop is hit, but the high of the day is 599p (although it could have been 602p, 610p or 620p for the purposes of this example). Later that day the stock reverses and by the close, it looks as if it is establishing a swing high rather than a change in trend.

A stop loss to exit the position could have been placed at 581p on the basis that that point would represent an outside day reversal. The share should at the very latest have been sold on the close at 562p. The share could also have been shorted on the close. It was indeed making a swing high, and it subsequently fell to 462p.

Note Although you will see these intraday reversals, and they will cost you money, this particular trade was easy to avoid. I have shown it purely as a good example of the intraday reversal. In fact the FTSE was in a clear bear market as a result of the Russian debt default, and it had rallied on 21st and 22nd September. It seemed very likely that the FTSE was about to complete a 3 day swing high on 23rd September (which is what it did). All one needed to do was to wait and see whether the FTSE itself breached its previous swing high (in which case one could buy one of its leading components BT) or whether, as was more likely, the bear trend would continue. There was no need to jump the gun by buying BT on the apparent breach of the swing high. Hindsight, I hear you say. Not a bit. See Chapter 10 on the benefits of cross-checking. This is a prime example of it.

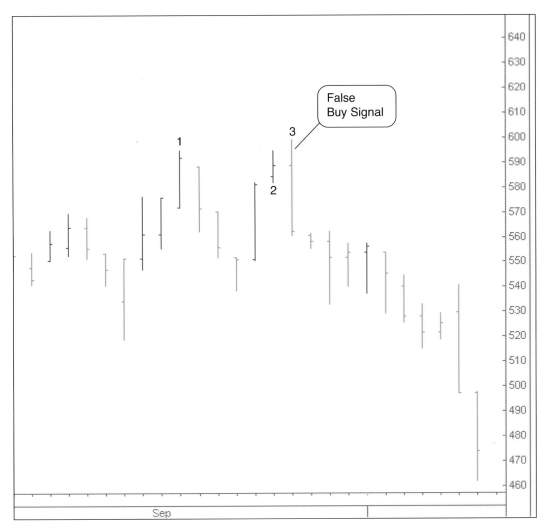

fig 4.15

Spring Trap Reversals

I was sure I had a book in my study by an American author which described one of his favourite reversal patterns as the Spring Trap Reversal, but I've been unable to find it, and therefore to give credit for it. In any event the genesis of this signal is clear enough. Richard Wyckoff wrote about technical analysis at roughly the same time as W.D. Gann. One of the chart patterns which he highlighted was the 'spring' which occurs when a falling market breaches a support level, but either the same day or the next day rallies back above the support level. If it does so the same day, it is an intraday reversal, as described above. The opposite of the spring is the upthrust which occurs when a rising market breaches resistance, only to fall back below the resistance within a short space of time.

The spring trap reversal is merely a type of Wyckoff spring/upthrust. It is similar to the intraday reversal, except that there is no indication on the day of the signal that anything is amiss. The classic spring trap reversal occurs the day after the swing chart buy or sell signal. Again the market is having second thoughts. There is in fact no new consensus developing about a change in trend.

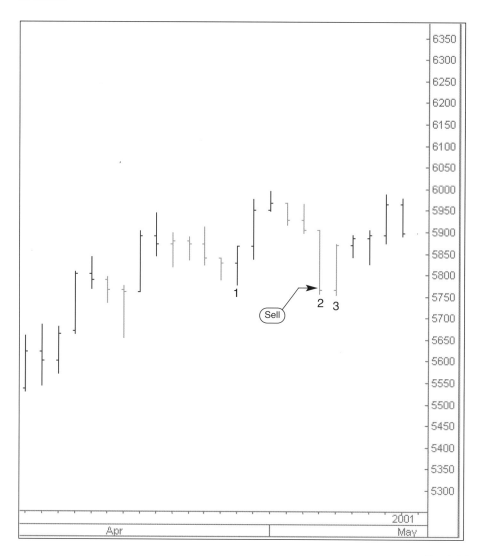

fig 4.16

1.   The FTSE swing low is made on 26th April 2001 at 5777, and the same day the market gives a buy signal as it rallies through the high of the previous day (5841).

2.   The move to new highs validates the putative swing low, but not much progress is made. In my style of trading (see Chapter 5), you would have taken half profits on your long

position at 5991, and you would have been stopped out of the remainder of your position at the entry point on 3rd May. The same day the FTSE plunges through the swing lows of 5777. The impression of a change in trend is reinforced by the very weak close, hard on the lows of the day.

3.   The following day the market opens a fraction higher, and then moves lower than the previous day but only by 1 point. After the weak close, following a sell signal, one expects a more substantial downside follow-through. The market rallies all day and closes on the highs of the day. The daily range (difference between high and low) is above average. The breach of the swing lows the previous day was a trap, as I noted on the web site I was writing for at the time.

Variations on the spring trap reversal

Look at the chart for FTSE in January 1999.

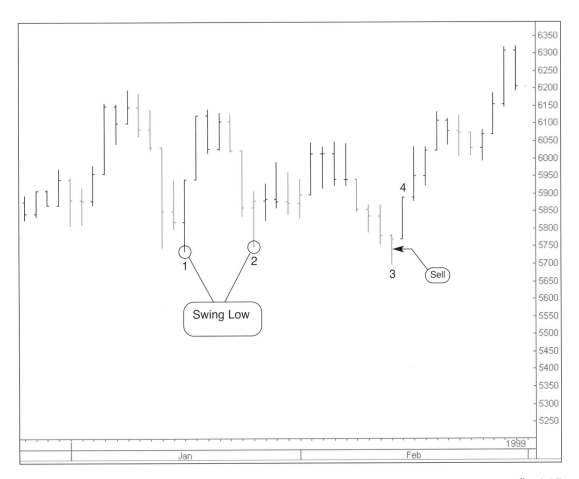

fig 4.17

1.   On 15th January the FTSE makes a swing low at 5737. The subsequent upward swing falls short of the early January highs.

2.   On 25th January the FTSE makes a fresh swing low at 5749, but again the subsequent upward swing falls short. FTSE is making an irregular pennant.

3.   On 10th February the FTSE opens at 5780. Sustained selling takes it clean through both swing lows down to 5698. A clear sell signal. Yet it rallies a bit by the close. At this point, one's brow furrows a little, but one can't be frightened out of a trade simply by this one unhelpful close.

4.   The next day, the reversal keeps going. Even at this stage, I am loathe to close out the trade. The market does manage to shake out weak holders in this fashion. But by the close I no longer need convincing. Throw in the towel.

I don't want to make too much of these false signals. You should not be frightened out of a trade at the first whiff of grapeshot. If in doubt, hold the position with your stop in place.

False spring trap reversals

If the spring trap reversal describes a false move, this is a false false move. Happily they are very rare beasts. This is the only clear example I could find in the FTSE index. Take the FTSE chart for May/June 1999, part of which I considered on page 33.

1.   The market rallies 445 points in 4 days making a very clear swing high. As it falls below the previous days low, it generates a clear sell signal. The sell signal is validated by the fact that the market makes new lows. Once again half profits of 150 points would have been taken.

2.   31st May. First up day. Stopped out of remaining half short position at the entry point.

3.   1st June. Inside day. Ignore.

4.   2nd June. Second up day.

5.   3rd June. Outside day with higher close. Counts as an up day. From this point, the swing trader is alert for a new sell signal, but the market continues to rally. Each day the stop sell order is moved up to underneath the previous days lows. But the sell order is never activated.

6.   On 7th June, the market rallies straight through swing high of 23rd May at 6462. Buy at 6463 stop. There is no follow-through that day. Market closes at 6432, which is not good but not worrying as yet.

7.   8th June. Market does edge a little higher, and closes at 6453, but still no follow-through.

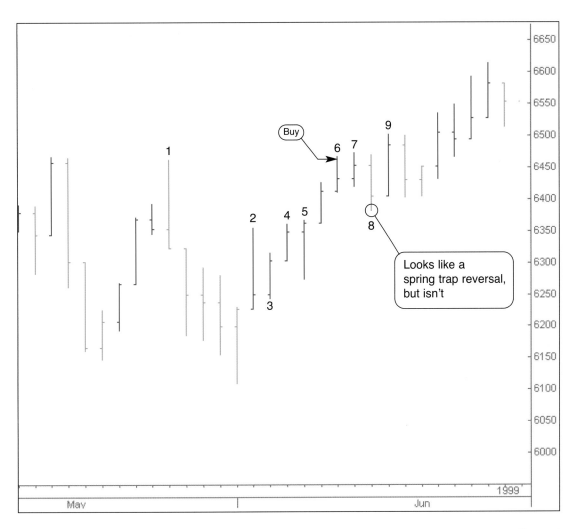

fig 4.18

8. 9th June. Down day with expanding daily range, closing near the lows of the day. Spring trap reversal. Sell at 6403 for 60pt loss.

9. 10th June. What!! Deeply unsporting. Market zooms ahead as if there never had been any cause to fret. Re-establish longs at 6470 with stop loss below lows of 9th June. Powerful finish to the day. Uptrend re-affirmed. Even then the market gives you a scare the very next day but the stop loss holds, and the market goes on to rally to 6614.

Tailpiece

The response I've had from the seminars I have given has been enthusiastic, although some have said that they found it a bit complicated. It can seem complicated because it is new. But swing charting is simplicity itself. Practise by back testing the principles on the market you follow most closely. Do not be put off by spring trap reversals which I have included for the sake of completeness. They are rare. They probably happen about once a year on average. You could entirely ignore the concept of spring trap reversals - simply hold your position with a 2.5% stop loss in place, and you won't need to worry about what is or is not a spring trap reversal. This approach may cost you a bit more money, but you will fret less.

The only really tricky part of my modified swing charts is distinguishing between a false start/complex swing and a change of trend, when the market spends just 2-4 days above the putative swing low and then crashes through it (vice versa for swing high).

As I mentioned on page 55, my rule of thumb is that if the market has spent 3 days above its swing low, and crashes through on the 4th day, it's a change of trend. That is easy enough. But frustratingly it can and does happen that the market spends 2 full days above its swing low and the best part of the third day above it as well, only to crash through the swing low right near the close of the third day. Now what? Does one stick rigidly to the rule of thumb? The answer is no, no rigidity. Intermarket cross checking, and looking at other indicators, such as (but not necessarily confined to) point & figure charts, usually clarifies the position. I explain this in the next chapter, and in Chapter 9. But I accept that it is a tricky part of the analysis. I like a challenge.

5 SWING CHARTING TACTICS

- My approach

- Profit maximisation techniques
    Stop losses
    Setting profit targets
    Linear phases

- Trading all the swings

My approach

Choose the right security

My 3bar/1 bar swing charts work well with most stock indices. I tend to stick to the FTSE 100, the Dow, NASDAQ (I chart both the Composite index and the trading vehicle, the NASDAQ 100), DAX and S&P 500, in approximately that order. They also work well with the high volatility, high volume stocks i.e. the TMT sector, the financials (banks and insurers), and basic materials. Since that is quite enough to cope with I don't bother with anything else.

Choose the right moment

I trade nearly all the swings which occur in the FTSE 100 and the Dow during the course of the year. An example of how lucrative this can be is contained at the end of this chapter. Why do I say 'nearly' all the swings? Because there are three occasions when I desist.

1.   **It is dangerous to initiate a position much after 7th December each year**. Just as newspapers have their silly season in the summer when there are no politicians to lampoon, so the stock market has a silly season in December. Hedge fund traders and fund managers who have secured their bonuses do not want to risk them. Even those who have fared less well do not want to make any big mistakes so late in the year. Make a mistake in January and you have 11 months to redeem yourself. Make a mistake in December and the sands of time have run out. Exaggerated price movements are often seen in December which are quickly reversed. Chart signals in the second half of December are particularly unreliable.

2.   **I will not initiate a new short position if the 5 week RSI is oversold**. I will not initiate a new long position if the 5 week RSI is overbought. You can read this chapter without knowing the detail underlying this rule, which is to be found at the end of Chapter 10.

3.   As mentioned in the last chapter **there are occasions when the charts appear equivocal, at least in real-time**. This is particularly so when the market rallies through a swing high (or falls through a swing low) which was established just 2 or 3 days earlier. Some might say this difficulty is my own creation since I have bent Gann's rules to allow for complex swing highs and lows to be formed instead of sticking to a rigid mechanical formula. I plead guilty, but without remorse. I believe complex swing highs and lows are a reality. The added flexibility which allows me to identify them and trade them as swing highs and lows is, I believe, a huge advantage. The price attached to that advantage is the occasional ambivalent picture. Intermarket cross checking, which I deal with immediately below, helps me make a decision. But if both intermarket cross checking and an examination of my point & figure charts does not help me reach a firm conclusion about whether the market is making a complex swing high or changing trend, I will liquidate my existing short position (just in case it is a change of trend), but I will not establish a new long position. So there is a tiny number of change of trend signals which I do not trade. I feel quite comfortable about this. When in doubt, stay out is a well-known market aphorism.

Intermarket Cross Checking

One of the most important tools in analysing an equivocal presentation on the chart is to look at allied markets or allied shares. A particularly good example of an intermarket clue occurred in February 2002. On 12th February the FTSE chart gave a sell signal after a 4 day rally, but then turned around as strength in the Dow led the market higher. On 14th February the FTSE powered through the putative swing high. Was this a change in trend? According to the rule of thumb that the market should stay below its swing high for at least 3 days before a breach of a swing high denotes a change in trend, this did look like a false start (which is what it turned out to be). But the FTSE had closed above its 20 day moving average, and the minor 25pt point & figure chart had generated a buy signal. So in real time, there was room for some doubt if one looked purely at the FTSE chart.

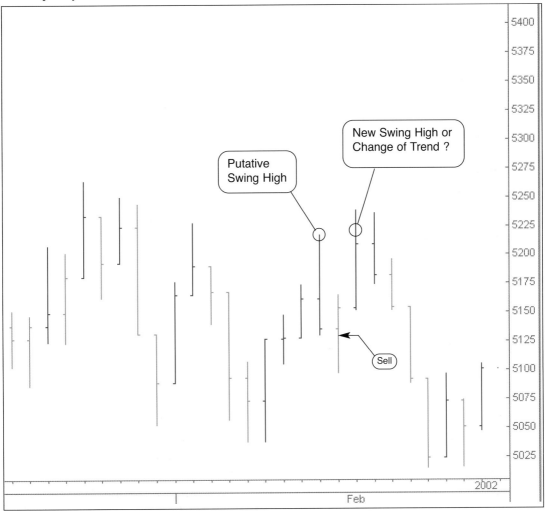

fig 5.1

But all one had to do was look at the S&P and NASDAQ charts. Not only were they in clear downtrends but they were miles away from the previous swing highs (unlike the FTSE). It was very likely that they were completing a 4 day rally. There was no indication to buy the S&P and the NASDAQ (fig 5.2), and indeed every indication that a fresh sell signal was about to be generated. At its highest, the NASDAQ and S&P might eventually turn around, but it would take some time. Answer: Doubts about the FTSE swing high are dispelled. Sure enough the NASDAQ and S&P did break to new lows, dragging the FTSE down.

fig 5.2

Likewise, if you are trading in banking shares and a particular bank looks like it is setting itself up for a swing chart buy signal, ask yourself what the other banks are doing. There is no need to try to tease a particular meaning out of a chart. There are often plenty of clues from the charts of related shares or markets.

Profit maximisation techniques

There are three additional devices which I use to maximise profits from trading index futures and options on swing charting principles:

- **Moving my stop losses up to my entry point**

- **Setting profit targets**

- **Doubling up during linear phases**

A. Stop losses

Initial stop losses

(i) Continuation of trend signals

With a continuation of trend signal, the place to put one's stop loss is obvious - just above the putative swing high if selling short or just below the putative swing low if going long.

I place the stop loss as soon as my new position is initiated. If it turns out the next day or the day after that it is a false start (market moves against you the very next day, continuing to form its swing high/low) I will be stopped out. I will wait for the new swing/high low to finish its formation before re-entering my short (or long) position.

(ii) Change of trend signals

With a change of trend signal, there is often no good place to put a stop loss. Quite often the market makes a peak and then changes trend by crashing through a previous swing low, without having first made a lower high. The stop loss on the newly entered short position should be placed above the old highs, but frequently that old high is miles away. It can make the risk/reward ratio hopelessly lopsided. A good example is the FTSE in January 1994 (fig 5.3). After making a new all-time high, it plummetted straight through the swing low of 28th January at 3402, giving a clear change of trend signal (and one that was to lead to a 15% fall in the market). The stop loss should have been placed above the old highs at 3540, but many traders would feel uncomfortable with a stop loss of just over 4%.

fig5.3

There are 3 solutions:

1. Liquidate your existing position but don't initiate a new position based on the change of trend signal. This is my least favourite option.

2. Place an arbitrary stop loss, consonant with the risk you're prepared to take e.g. a stop loss say 2.5% away even though there is no relevant chart point at that level.

3. Trade the change of trend signal by using an option or option spread e.g. instead of selling futures as I would do on a continuation of trend signal, I buy a put option or a bear spread. That fixes your potential loss. It also has the very great advantage that on those few occasions that there is a (false) hint of a spring trap reversal, one is not panicked out of the position.

Traders should choose whichever option best suits their risk profile. Nowadays I use a combination of 2 and 3 above.

Moving stop losses

As the Maginot line proved, fixed defences have their limitations. My stop losses do not remain fixed.

When a false or failed signal happens, I am quite sanguine about it. You've got to get used to taking losses. They are inevitable.

When I deduce that the market is headed in a particular direction, and I put on an appropriate position and it does head in that direction, I am content. The swing chart has 'worked'. But since the chart describes only an imbalance of supply and demand, and future events may rectify that imbalance, even turn it the other way, I find that chart signals have limited durability, unless the market is in a linear phase.

It sets my teeth on edge when substantial profits evaporate and I ultimately lose money on what has been a (briefly) successful chart signal.

The great traders of yore said: never let a profit run into a loss.

Whilst it is impossible to follow that stricture literally, I do follow it in spirit.

> (i) Continuation of trend signals
>
> In all non-linear phases, as a general rule, I move my stop loss up to my entry point when the FTSE has moved 100 points in my favour. This does result in my being stopped out needlessly on a handful of occasions but mostly it saves me a lot of money. I do the same for the Dow when it has moved more than 180 points in my favour.
>
> When I perceive (rightly or wrongly) a linear phase, I will move my stop loss on my regular position as soon as the market moves 100 points in my favour, but I will not move my stop loss on my linear phase position. This is explained below.
>
> (ii) Change of trend signals
>
> With swing charts (and point & figure charts) there is often a little stutter before a change in trend really gets going, so with change of trend signals, I give the market a little time (3 clear days after the day of the signal) to prove itself before moving my stop loss to the entry level after the FTSE has moved 100 points in my favour (180 points for the Dow).

Moving stop losses with individual equities

Likewise when I trade individual equities, I am quick to move up my stop. Of course this is a mental stop since the electronic order book will not accept stop orders. Alternatively, if I'm in Court, I leave the stop order with my broker/spreadbetting firm on a "not held basis". I calculate when to move my stop loss to the entry point on the individual equities by a bit of back testing, but it tends to be after the market has moved about 6-7% in my favour.

I regard moving my stop loss as a vital tactic for successful swing trading. Whether or not you accept the detail of the above "rules" about moving your stop loss, I do suggest you embrace the principle.

B. Setting profit targets

At this point I commit something of a heresy. I take profits early. One is always told to run one's profits and cut one's losses. Certainly losses must be cut, but swing charting is such a short term device that I've found that taking profits early makes little difference to one's bottom line. When the markets are in a linear phase one can indeed run one's profits. But linear phases are rare. You will get one, maybe two a year. There are long passages of time in each year when the market is either in a choppy sideways phase or it is trending very gently up or down with occasional sharp breaks.

Back testing

Before I go on to the subject of profit targets, and what may or may not be achievable with swing charts, I should deal briefly with back testing. Any trader should be able to write down on a single piece of A4 paper the broad parameters which will lead him to enter and exit positions. 'Buy when I think its going up' does not qualify. If you can't write down what makes you buy and sell, you had better be lucky or an intuitive genius. Once you have a broad method, back test it on the charts. If you are using moving averages or any of the popular arithmetical indicators, you can back test by using the optimiser facility which most modern software possesses.

Back testing won't prove that you will definitely make money, but it may prove that you won't. What is more it will reveal which securities are not susceptible to the type of analysis or chart method you intend to use. Swing charting will definitely not work on every stock (see below).

I have back tested the swing charts on the FTSE index from 1985 onwards and the results reveal an annual return of as low as 6% and as high as 42%.

This may seem disappointing to some, but it is not to me. Most of the results fall in the 12-24% range. With the benefit of leverage which futures, options and CFDs provide, an unleveraged yield of 6-42% is perfectly acceptable in my view. In any event, I try to boost the return by increasing my position in linear phases (see opposite).

Wealth warning: Back testing does not indicate what is likely to be achieved. It indicates the *maximum* which is achievable. There is a massive psychological component to trading the markets. If you don't know what I mean, you'll find out in due course. Inexperienced traders will consistently do worse than backtested results and even experienced traders will only occasionally match such results. Back testing merely gives a rudimentary idea of what is possible.

The right target

I doubt that there is a single fixed profit target that is right for every phase of the market, year in year out. Selecting a profit target is something you need to tinker with continuously. The profitable FTSE signals in the years 1999 to 2001 were as follows:

Gain	100-149	150-199	200-249	250-299	300-399	400+
1999	5	2	2	2	5	0
2000	4	3	3	3	4	1
2001	1	3	6	0	2	2

Each buy and sell signal has been counted from the point it was triggered to the lowest/highest point of that move before there was another swing high/low or change in trend.

As a matter of experience, I find that the best targets for me are 150 points and 300 points on the FTSE. In non-linear situations, I take half profits invariably when the market has moved 150 points in my favour. I take full profits somewhere between 150-300 points. I tend to play it by ear as to when exactly I get out. Taking modest half profits never bothers me. I like putting money in the bank.

Reliability

For the sake of completeness, I should also deal with the failures: failed signals, false signals and false starts. In the last 3 years, the following losing trades were recorded in the FTSE.

	Change of trend signals	Continuation of trend signals
1999	3 out of 8	6 out of 16
2000	1 out of 10	7 out of 16
2001	3 out of 7	3 out of 13

That looks very good doesn't it? An accuracy rate of two out of three. It is half true. If you're looking at it from the point of view of how many trades made losses, it was indeed one in three. But some of the successful trades did not make me any money, because I raised my stop loss to the entry point after the market had moved more than 100 points in my favour, and my stop loss was later hit. Sometimes I was right to do so, sometimes not. I haven't re-calculated the accuracy rate to take account of those occasions because it seems to me that those occasions should be counted as a success. The swing chart signals worked. My profit objectives suited my risk profile, but someone who had smaller expectations (say 100 points per trade) would have profited on all of those occasions.

C. Linear phases

I use the term 'linear phase' as a shorthand way of describing that phase of the market when a substantial move unfolds. The signature of a linear phase is a substantial change in price over several weeks or months, during part of which time the price movement resembles a straight line. Obviously the swing trader is keen to capture as much as possible of such a move.

Linear phases are very often connected to a theme, like 'Enronitis'. I can't think of a reliable way of identifying all linear phases in advance. If anyone could identify linear phases in advance, they would sit out all the difficult phases of the market, and roll in money every time a linear phase presented itself. But I have found one mechanical way of catching many linear phases. The following is a method I use to increase the size of my position upon the assumption that a linear movement may be in the offing.

The first continuation of trend signal after a change in trend often yields the best profits. If there is going to be a long run, that first countertrend move is the one to watch for.

It is clear from analysis of swing charts that some change of trend of signals can be treacherous, hence the discussion about intraday reversal and spring trap reversals. They can also be very profitable. But if a change of trend signal is going to be short-lived, it will seldom go on to give any continuation of trend signals. If there is a false change in trend signal or an embryonic change in trend about which the market has second thoughts, this usually shows up early in the charts - usually within days. But when you do see a continuation of trend signal which follows a change in trend signal, it is an important milestone in the development of the trend.

W.D. Gann was of the same view. It was at this stage of the trend that he was keen on pyramiding, as he called it. Effectively, I assume that any market which has given both a change of trend signal and a continuation of trend signal is about to set off on a long profitable run. I then double up my position (or at any rate increase it substantially). Naturally this assumption is not always borne out, but it is seldom costly. I set out here a subset of rules to capitalise on potential linear phases.

Linear phase rules

Rule 1

Look for the *first* countertrend swing of at least 3 days *after* a change in trend signal, in line with swing charting principles.

Some sort of filter is needed to exclude those continuation of trend signals where the market doesn't really have the momentum to set off on a long run. I am sure a variety of indicators can be used. I use a 14 day moving average, which is short enough to give some idea of short-term momentum although not too short to turn on an extended countertrend rally.

Rule 2

After the 3 day countertrend move has been identified, check by referring to the close that the 14 day moving average is still moving in the direction of the supposed trend.

Note that since the trade will be put on the following day, this indicator effectively lags by one day. You'll see what I mean below. Note also that it is purely the slope of the moving average which is important. For these purposes, it is irrelevant whether the market price is above or below the moving average.

What stop loss rule should be employed? Clearly in a linear phase one wants to hang in for a long run. At the same time with a doubled up position, one is vulnerable to making a double helping of losses. So I adopt a hybrid position. I set a profit target of 200 points on one position, my normal position size, and I move my stop loss to the entry point as soon as the market has moved more than 100 points in my favour. In other words I treat it much the same as a normal swing. Then I take an increased position (up to double in total) on the linear phase. On this position, I do not move my stop loss. I am willing to take the extra risk for the extra benefit because linear phases can be so lucrative.

Rule 3

Do not move your stop loss to entry point on linear phase element of your position.

Rule 4

Do not take any new positions between 7 December and 31 December.

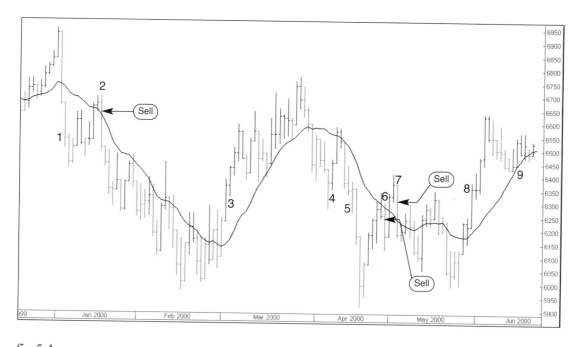

fig 5.4

Apply that to the years 2000 and 2001 on the FTSE

Max Profit/Actual loss

1.   5.1.00 Change of trend to down.

2.   18.1.00 First countertrend rally. 14 day moving average (M14) is still   **+664pts**
      moving lower as of 17.1.00. Market rallies shortly after opening to make
      new highs. Place sell stop at 6637 under lows of 17.1.00. Stop triggered later
      on 18.1.00.

3.   1.3.00 Change of trend to up as complex swing high of 24.2.00 is taken out
      on the fourth day after the swing high was made. No countertrend dips on
      this upswing. So even though, with hindsight, this did turn out to be a brief
      but steep linear phase, it would not have been identified as such. No
      mechanical method is perfect.

4.   6.4.00 M14 not satisfied. The moving average was falling on 5th (and 6th)
      April. Filter works successfully as this signal ultimately fails.

5.   13.4.00 Change of trend to down.

6. 27.4.00 Apparent first countertrend rally but it's a false start.   **-96pts**

7. 3.5.00 Now the swing high is formed. M14 is satisfied. Sell short at 6311   **+319pts**
    below the low of 2.5.00.

8. 30.5.00 Change of trend to up as swing high of 16.5.00 is taken out.

9. 13.6.00 First countertrend dip. Everything sets up perfectly for a new linear   **-51pts**
    phase but the market does not oblige. After limping upwards for 7 days, it
    flops through the stop loss. A failed signal.

fig 5.5

10. 22.6.00 Change of trend to down.

11. 11.7.00 First countertrend rally. M14 satisfied, but it's a false start.   **-54pts**

12. 13.7.00 By the time the real swing high has been established, M14 not
     satisfied; it is rising so this swing would have traded as an ordinary swing,
     not a linear phase, which is just as well because a normal, rather than a
     supernormal, profit was all that was available.

13.   16.8.00 (Confirmed by a very clear signal from the point & figure chart.) Change of trend to up, but after a sharp 2 week rally there is an equally sharp plunge and no countertrend dip clearly presents itself.

14.   14.9.00 is an equivocal signal, but any thought of a linear phase would have been countermanded by M14 which was falling. The trend changes back to down on 18.9.00.

15.   9.10.00 First countertrend rally. M14 satisfied. Sell short at 6341.   **+324pts**

16.   24.10.00 Change of trend from down to up.

17.   14.11.00 First countertrend dip, but M14 not satisfied. No linear phase develops so the filter works correctly again.

Analysis: The main linear phase of 2000 (January/February) was captured well. The second linear phase (March) was not, but it was brief. Trading the change of trend of signal meant that a profit would indeed have been made, but not on a doubled up position. Two other reasonable swings were captured. There was one modest failed signal costing 51 points. There were 2 false starts which would have been avoided by a 2 bar trigger for the buy/sell signal. But waiting for that second bar would have cost, over the year as a whole, much more than actual 150 points loss on the false starts.

So far I have just set out the maximum profit available. How do you actually realise these profits? Frankly I tend to play it by ear when I'm in an assumed linear phase. I take half profits virtually automatically at about the 200 point level and run the remaining position with an eye on the RSI (see Chapter 10). You could, however, use a mechanical method for realizing profits. An example is:

Rule 5

After the market has moved 200 points in your favour, take profits on the third day the FTSE crosses the Bollinger Band.

On the next page, I have applied a 21 day weighted Bollinger Band set at 2 standard deviations to the FTSE chart so that you can see the application of this rule.

For the year 2000, the results are good:

- You get out the day of the low of the entire January/February linear movement and close to the lows in the other 2 swings.

- You capture 627 points on the 18.1.00 sell signal, 271 points on the 3.5.00 sell signal and

246 points on the 17.10.00 signal.

• Net profit for the year on linear phases = 943pts equivalent to about 15% on the linear phase element alone.

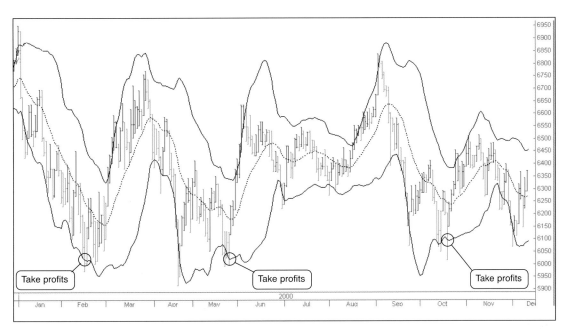

fig 5.6

In the powerful downward linear phase of June/July 2002, the Bollinger Band rule would not have worked nearly so well. A gain of 474 points would have been achieved, which is not bad at all. But it was less than half of the 1000 points on offer during that linear phase. You will find that the same applies if you back test rigorously my Bollinger Band rule over a decade or more. Some years it works brilliantly, other years it gets you out too early and in yet other years it fails to get you out at all because the linear phase ends after only 2 crosses of the Bollinger Band. I've mentioned this "rule" to feed the powerful desire of investors and traders for a metric. The truth is I doubt that there is a single mechanical way, applicable to all kinds of markets, which will close out a successful position at just the right time.

Now the year 2001.

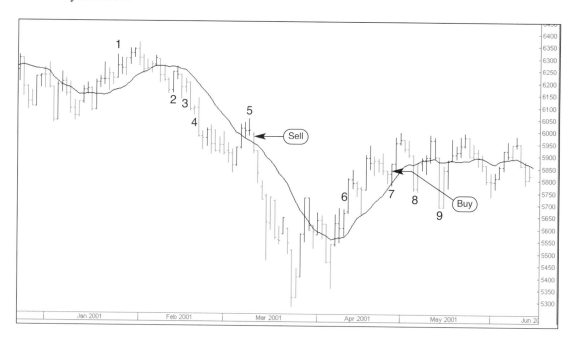

fig 5.7

1. 24.1.01 Change of trend from down to up as swing high of 2.1.01 and possible swing high of 19.1.01 is breached.

2. 12.2.01 First countertrend dip. M14 not satisfied. Filter works well, as no linear phase (or profit of any kind) materialises.

3. 14.2.01 Possible change in trend.

4. 20.2.01 Definite change in trend.

5. 9.3.01 First countertrend rally. M14 satisfied. Sell short at 5981(underneath lows of 8.3.01)   **+701pts**

6. 10.4.01 Change of trend from down to up.

7. 25.4.01 First countertrend dip. M14 satisfied. Buy at 5841. Later stopped out.   **-65pts**

8. 3.5.01 False change of trend signal.

9. 13.5.01 LSE closing auction fiasco. Ignore. Trend still up.

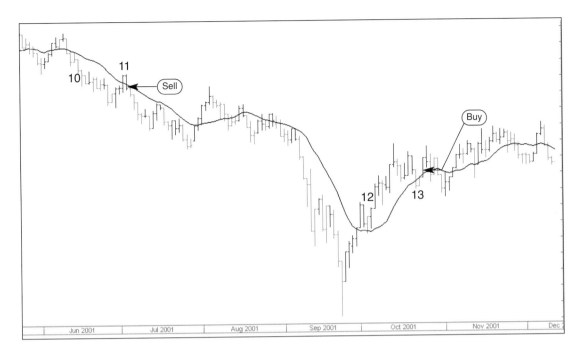

fig 5.8

10. 14.6.01 Change of trend from up to down.

11. 3.7.01 First countertrend rally. M14 satisfied. Sell short at 5629. **+733pts**

12. 4.10.01 Change of trend from down to up.

13. 23.10.01 First countertrend dip M14 satisfied. Buy at 5079. Later stopped **-76pts**
     out.

Analysis: Both linear phases are captured well. The second linear phase was in fact worth a maximum of not 733 points but 1409 points. However I decline to count profits after 11th September.

Now applying the Bollinger Band rule, it works well with the second linear phase, getting one out of the market on the very day of the low (10th September), capturing 595 points. It doesn't work so well on the March linear phase but still manages to capture 404 points. Net profit for the year on linear phases = 766 points, equivalent to a return of about 13% on the linear phase element alone.

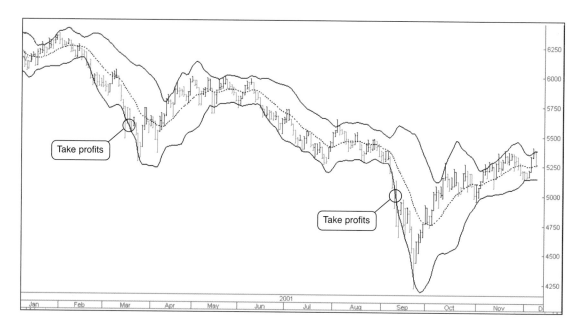

fig 5.9

Trading tip: I have put forward a 14 day moving average as a filter to exclude some of the first continuation of trend signals which do not appear to have the oomph to turn into linear phases. Another, more imprecise, filter which I use is the level at which the first continuation of trend signal occurs. If the first continuation of trend buy signal occurs above the point at which the change of trend buy signal occurs, that is obviously a good sign. The market has held onto its gains, and it is giving a repeat buy signal at a higher level, which is clearly indicative of the enthusiasm of the buyers. If the first continuation of trend buy signal occurs at the same level as the change of trend signal or even slightly below it, it is plainly less emphatic than one would like, but still OK in my opinion. But where the first continuation of trend buy signal occurs more than 3% below the original buy signal, I am deeply sceptical that any linear phase will unfold. It is hardly a rampant bull market that gives up all of the gains it has made on the change of trend signal, and then loses 3% more before giving a repeat buy signal.

Trading all the swings

Thus far I have concentrated on 3 techniques which I use in an attempt to maximise profits, namely trading linear phases, moving my stop loss to the entry point at an early stage and booking half profits early. As you've already seen, catching the linear phases can make a tremendous difference to a trader's bottom line. However it is not only the linear phases which one should trade. Trading all the swings is profitable although there can be long phases in which it is a bit of a grind (the FTSE in January to April 2002 being an irritatingly good example). In this section I set out a typical example of how one might trade all the swings.

NASDAQ 100

The NASDAQ has caused much sorrow to traders, but see below how uncomplicated it was to trade all the swings. On this occasion I have used the NASDAQ 100 over the 12 months prior to writing this chapter (late April 2001 to end April 2002). In order not to complicate matters, I have run the example without doubling up on the linear phases. I have assumed a 2 contract position for the purposes of taking half profits.

Rules

a. In non-linear phases take half profits on a gain of 100 points and half profits on remaining position on a gain of 140 points.

b. In linear phases, take half profits on a gain of 140 points, and run remaining position until the 5 day RSI falls below 14 or rises above 86 (the RSI is a momentum indicator which I use as a tool for taking profits. It is explained in Chapter 10. For the moment, you'll just have to take it on trust), or until the trend changes, whichever occurs soonest.

c. Raise/lower stop to entry level after 4 days, provided market has moved 100 points or more in your favour.

d. Do not initiate any new positions whilst weekly RSI is below 18 or above 82.

e. Where there is no obvious close swing high or low, use a stop loss of 80 points.

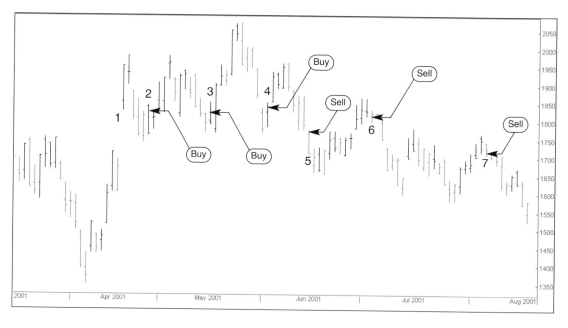

fig 5.10

1. 19th April. There is a clear change of trend as market makes a huge gap opening above the previous swing highs. Although I will activate positions on gap openings, this one is so large that it would be impossible to do so. There would be no sensible place to put a stop loss. Wait for continuation of trend signal.

2. 26th April. Buy on (gap) opening at 1839 as market exceeds previous swing high of 1825. In this instance there is a sensible, if distant, place to put a stop loss (underneath the putative swing low at 1743). Potential linear phase. Take half profits of 140 points on 2nd May. Stopped out of remaining position at entry point on 4th May. Although the activation of this stop loss seems wrong because the market later goes up, no linear phase does in fact eventuate.

3. 15th May. Buy at 1821 as market takes out highs of 14th May. Later take profits of 100 and 140 points.

4. 1st June. Buy at 1838. Take half profits of 100 points. Stopped out of remaining position at entry point.

5. 14th June. Sell short at 1766 as market changes trend by breaching lows of 30 May. Take half profits of 100 points. Stopped out of remaining position at entry point.

6. 3rd July. Sell short at 1814. Potential linear phase. Take half profits of 140 points and then 460* points on 7th September 2001 on the RSI reading.

7. 3rd August. Sell short at 1717. Later take profits of 100 and 140 points.

fig 5.11

8. 29th August. Sell short at 1525. Later take profits of 100 and 140 points.

9. 24th and 25th September are up days. 26th September is a down day. 28th is an up day. A swing chart sell signal is generated on 29th September. Stopped out for 80 point loss.

10. 3rd October. Until just prior to the close, the NASDAQ had spent 3 days under the putative swing low. Although this looks like a buy signal, it is admittedly not crystal clear from the swing chart alone. In fact the point & figure chart of the NASDAQ Comp gave my favourite buy signal on this very day (see page 93), so I never was in much doubt. Buy at 1257. Later take profits of 100 and 140 points. Hereafter one is looking keenly for a 3 day swing low to trade a linear phase. But it never quite happens. There are several 2 day setbacks in the course of October and November, but no 3 day setbacks. It is clear by the end of November that the occasion for a linear phase has gone. No trading after 10th December. In any event, the weekly RSI is over 79. The chart is quite murky thereafter.

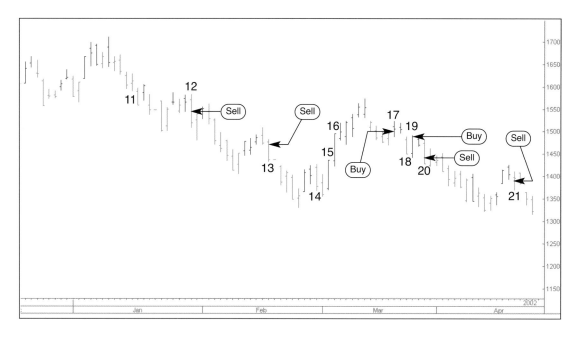

fig 5.12

11.   Come early January, it is a bit of a puzzle. It is not clear what is the trend. The plunge on 20th December could be interpreted as a swing low in an uptrend, or more reasonably 20th December turned the trend down. There were enough days (3) above the swing lows to satisfy my rule of thumb about change of trend signals, but there was no follow-through. A clue is provided on 11th January when the 10pt point & figure chart generates a sell signal, but since this is a swing chart model I won't count that. Matters are made clear on 18th January as the market breaks its December lows. This must be a downtrend. But it is too late to act on a change of trend signal. The market is merely revealing that the previous equivocal position was in fact a downtrend. Wait for a continuation of trend signal which should be a linear phase.

12.   24th January is an up day. 25th January is a down day. 26th January is an up day. 29th January does have a higher high, giving one the signal to put a stop sell order below the lows of 26th January. But its high remains below the high of 24th January. I mentioned this problem in the section on complex swings on page 42 and on page 44. In this sort of position I would take a half position because:

a. 29th turns out to be an outside day, and the highs of the 29th and 24th are fairly close.
b. If the market had set up perfectly, this would have been a linear phase.
c. The Dow gave a classic continuation of trend sell signal on 29th January.

Later take profits of 140 points.

13.   15th February. Sell short at 1470. Later take profits of 100 and 140 points.

14.   On 25th, 26th and 27th February the market does rally, and ordinarily one would have gone short on 27th February but the weekly RSI is at 16.8, so this sell signal is not acted upon.

15.   1st March. Market moves through highs of 27th February. Equivocal presentation. Could be a change in trend buy signal or just a swing high in the making, especially since the weekly RSI is oversold (until the close that day). Do nothing.

16.   By 5th March, as the market breaches the swing high of 14th February, it becomes clear that the move on 1st March was in fact a change in trend, but its too late to act on that. Instead look for the first continuation of trend signal for a linear phase position.

17.   18th March. Buy at 1499. This potential linear phase does not work out.

18.   20th March. Is this a change of trend or a complex swing low in the making? Not clear. Stop loss on linear phase position activated below the putative swing lows at 1469, but don't go short (pity) because picture unclear.

19.   21st March. Clarity is achieved. This looks like a swing low after the market bounces off its lows, and closes up firmly after an outside day. Buy at 1489. But do not confuse clarity with accuracy. It is not a swing low. The market continues to decline. Stopped out under the putative swing low (1442) on 25th March.

20.   25th March. This cannot any longer be the same swing low forming in an uptrend. It must be a change of trend signal. That impression is confirmed by the Dow which has already given a very clear change of trend signal. Sell short at 1442. Later take profits of 100 and 140 points.

21.   18th April. Potential linear phase. Sell short at 1392. Later take profits of 140 points and 231 points on 6th May when an RSI reading of 12.2 is obtained.

*In fact the RSI reached only 15.5 on 7th September, so according to the above the rules this linear phase position would have been held through 11th September and a much bigger profit would have resulted, but I decline to count that windfall.

Analysis

a. Linear phases: There were 2 attempts to trade the same linear phase in mid-March. I count that as one failure costing a total of 107 points. There were 3 winners totalling 1111 points. Net gain 1004 points.

b. The non-linear swings had 1 loser costing 160 points and 8 winners totalling 1780 points for a net gain of 1620 points.

The net result is 2624 points, or the equivalent of 1312 points per contract, a return of close to 80% unleveraged over the period of one year and a bit. The accuracy rate of 11 winners to 2 losers is rather better than you should expect over the long term, but it does demonstrate how simple and profitable swing charting can be.

Of course, now that the NASDAQ 100 is trading below 900, my sights are lowered. One needs to take account of the fact that a 140 point move in the NASDAQ 100 now would be rather more than you could fairly expect from an ordinary swing. So my profit targets are now 60 and 90 points on regular swings.

Individual equities

If swing charts are so brilliant, why do I use point & figure charts as my main guide when swing trading individual equities?

You can successfully trade many high volatility, high volume stocks using swing charts only. But merely because swing charts are excellent seems little reason to ignore every other indicator. Swing charts are occasionally ambivalent.

Swing charting is profitable when applied to active stocks. There are many stocks which are too inactive for swing charting to be of any value. Even stocks in the FTSE 100 index which attract good daily levels of volume can be unsuited to swing charting. Many of the old economy stocks plod dolefully on, like Eeyore. Excellent long-term investments they may be (I even have a few of them in my self-select pension fund), but instead of taking 3-5 days to make swing lows they can often take weeks. They are much more inert.

Look at the chart of Reckitt Benckiser, one of the top 40 companies listed on the London Stock Exchange.

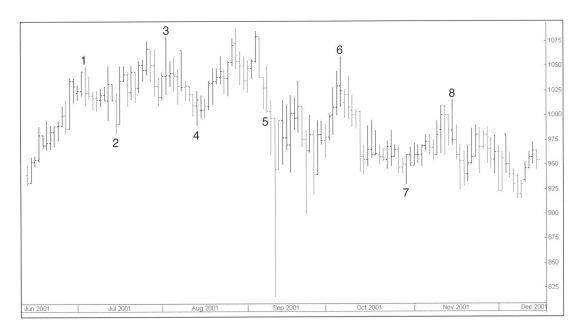

fig 5.13

1. The stock made a high on 3.7.01.

2. It took 8 days to make a new swing low on 13.7.01.

3. A new high was made on 1.8.01.

4. It took a further 8 days to make a a swing low at 990p on 13.8.01.

5. The swing low is breached on 10.9.01 leading to a sharp fall from which the share recovers.

6. It takes 17 days to make a new swing high on 4.10.01, generating a false buy signal whilst doing so.

7. 16 days pass before a new low is made on 29.10.01.

8. It took a further 12 days to make a swing high on 14.11.01.

The swings are plain to see, but my style of trading a 3 bar countertrend move/1 bar trading signal would not work with this stock. In Reckitt's case, a 6 bar countertrend move/2 bar trading signal might work. I don't know. I would guess that it is possible to devise a viable swing chart which varies with the volatility of a stock. Paritech (www.paritech.co.uk) market software known as Hot Trader which may be the best software on the market for swing charts. It is very versatile. You can stipulate various lengths of swing chart i.e. 1 bar, 2 bar, 3, 4 or 5 bar etc. What you cannot do, however, is stipulate a 6 bar swing to define the desired correction, and a 1 bar swing to activate the buy or sell signal, although I should imagine it would not be too difficult for the programmers to make that change.

I steer clear of stocks and securities that are not susceptible to my style of trading.

When trading individual equities, I have regard to both the swing chart and the point & figure chart and it is the point & figure chart which has primacy. But I want to make crystal clear that swing trading purely with swing charts can be successfully undertaken in individual equities.

In Appendix 2, I show how all the swings in Rio Tinto could have been successfully traded with swing charts for the 26 month period ending April 2002.

6 POINT & FIGURE CHARTS

- Introduction

- Ethos

Introduction

The origin of the term point & figure is shrouded in mystery. It is said to refer to the way grain merchants recorded prices in the late 19th Century.

The man who originally made point & figure famous was A.W. Cohen in his book *How to Use the 3-point Reversal Method of Point & Figure Stock Market Trading*, published by Chartcraft Inc. in 1947. It has been re-printed several times, but is now out of print. Michael L. Burke of Investors Intelligence is the spiritual successor to A.W. Cohen. Mr Burke remains one of the world's best known point & figure practitioners.

I do not want to bog down the text at this point with a detailed explanation of how to construct a point & figure chart, (see Appendix 1 if you want guidance on this) but I do need to deal with some aspects of construction because they are germane to interpretation. I also need to set out a brief glossary at this point so that the uninitiated can follow:

- *X* represents rising prices

- *O* represents falling prices

- *Box* The name originates from the squared paper on which point & figure charts are usually drawn. Each box is the unit of price movement chosen for that chart. Choosing a lower unit value makes the chart more sensitive and increases the number of signals, both good and bad. A higher value reduces the number of signals.

- *3 box reversal* It is usual (but not compulsory) to plot a new column representing a change in direction only when the price moves 3 boxes in the opposite direction. The point of this requirement is to eliminate minor moves which would otherwise clutter the chart without a corresponding benefit in interpretation. Effectively, all price movement which runs counter to the existing plotted direction but falls short of 3 boxes is deemed to constitute mere background noise.

- *No time scale* Point & figure charts are constructed 'under eternity' as A.W. Cohen's book rather grandly puts it. This means that there is no time axis. If a share price makes tiny oscillations for days on end without ever achieving a 3 box reversal there will be no addition to the chart. Effectively the X axis simply records, by columns of Xs and Os, the number of occasions upon which there has been a relevant reversal in price.

The only record of time in a point & figure chart is when an X or O is replaced with the number of the month. This occurs on the first addition to the chart made in the month. It is simply a reference point. Modern software will allow you to rest the cursor on any column of Xs or Os to see exactly when the price action took place.

Ethos

The point & figure chart is much loved by day traders and floor traders (they still exist in the US). It has stood the test of time. It is still very often the chart of choice for many technical analysts and traders despite the fact that much more sophisticated analysis can be done with PCs. Why?

- **Point & figure charts have a huge advantage which distinguishes them from most other charts.** *Every other chart measures time on the X axis thereby implicitly according equal weight to each day's price action. This is counterintuitive. Every trader knows that not all days are equally informative*; not all days have price action which is equally representative of the balance between the forces of supply and demand. The point & figure chart uniquely and automatically attempts to differentiate between the useful and the unimportant.

- Point & figure charting is not rocket science. The charts are easy to read and they are effective. The picture of supply and demand is very clear, which gives one confidence in the message conveyed. By contrast, many of the indicators available on charting software are purely arithmetical calculations. They are used because they have worked in the past when the market is trending, but they convey comparatively little in terms of supply and demand.

- Because the X axis does not measure time but only movement, the chart displays more clearly the change in volatility and interest in a particular stock. Write in the date on a point & figure chart and you will see that 20 columns can sometimes cover just a few weeks trading, other times it will cover a year's trading.

- Almost all other charts use the closing price of the day or the high low close of the day as a reference point. Since one cannot tell during the day what will be the high low and close, most charts are dynamically retarded by one day. But point & figure charts are often used in real time.

Strictly speaking it is not even necessary to have a computer with the requisite software on it. For years, I speculated only in the futures markets of bonds, gilts, the FTSE and the Dow Jones. All I needed was 4 hand-drawn charts and a helpful broker. I still keep half a dozen charts which I update manually every day (for the times when I am sent to some faraway court on circuit and will not be returning to my computer that night). It takes a total of about 5 minutes to complete the manual updating.

As I've mentioned, I do need to cover two important aspects of construction: 'Data to be used', and 'Box value'.

Data to be used

There are several different ways of constructing point & figure charts. A.W. Cohen was clear that point & figure charts were not to be based on closing prices. Yet when you use charting software, you will be offered the option of constructing the point & figure chart on the basis of the closing price. This is not as absurd as it sounds. In many illiquid stocks a single large purchase order can cause movement during the day which is not truly representative of the totality of the forces of supply and demand. As the market approaches the close and the buying order has been filled, the market edges back downwards. In those circumstances, the close may be more truly representative of the forces of supply and demand than the intraday trading.

The same does not apply to the most liquid 100 to 200 stocks where the intraday trading provides a valuable guide to the exact level where demand and supply are strongest. In the case of the most liquid stocks, those to which the swing trader would naturally gravitate, a real time chart is not only more accurate than a chart based on closing prices but also avoids some of the considerable perils that can exist in swing trading with a point & figure chart based on closing prices. See Appendix 1 for a description of these perils.

There is another method of construction which is intellectually unsatisfactory but is pragmatic. Much of the charting software on the market, if it has a point & figure function at all, will offer the choice of point & figure charts based on closing prices or on the daily high/low prices. By charting the high and low, the computer is attempting to mimic real time.

This slightly curious method of construction has led to the belief in some quarters that a point & figure chart cannot be constructed by adding more than one column per day. That is exactly what a computer does when it plots the chart based on the high and low price. It only ever adds to an existing column (if prices move in the same direction) or it adds one new column (if prices move in the opposite direction by a sufficient amount). But a computer plotting from the high and low price never adds to an existing column, as well as plotting a reversal on the same day even though that is exactly what may have happened to the share price. A share which opens way up on the day and declines all day will be recorded by the computer only as having advanced. The decline is not plotted. It is fanciful to suppose that that is the right way to construct a point & figure chart. There is no conceivable reason why an intraday reversal should be ignored - on the contrary, it will add to the picture of supply and demand, and any chart that does not show that intraday reversal is not telling the full story.

But in fact, the damage is minor. A real time chart and a chart based on high/low prices are more than 90% similar provided a big box size is used.

Best of all is the real time chart which shows you every point of supply and demand. I use a real time price feed, but I do make it clear that although a real time system is best, it is by no means compulsory. For the purposes of employing the principles in this book, an end-of-day system, which will plot only one column a day from the high/low price will work perfectly well.

Box value

This is a more important issue than most people realize. A.W. Cohen gave a detailed account of how the box value should change from $1 per box to 50c per box when the share fell through $20. It follows that when a share was trading at about $30 he was using a box value of about 3%, when it was trading at $90 he was using a box value of 1.1% and when it was trading at about $19, he was using a box value of about 2.5%. Be chary of using box values of much less than 1%.

I agree that the box value should be altered according to the level at which a share or index is trading. For example a 10pt or 20pt box is now appropriate for the NASDAQ Comp, but it would not have been appropriate when the Comp was trading over 4000.

A good illustration of the difference made by box size is provided by the NASDAQ Comp after it bounced off its lows in September 2001. The 20pt chart is perfect. Not a single false signal. The only failed signal comes as the market makes its peak in January 2002 and even it would have cost very little. In any event, losing money when the market turns is not unusual. As the NASDAQ falls once again the chart is as good as gold. This is point & figure charting at its very best. The individual buy and sell signals on this chart will be considered in Chapter 8.

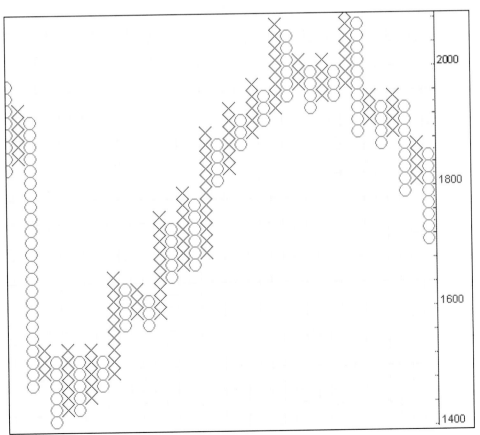

fig 6.1

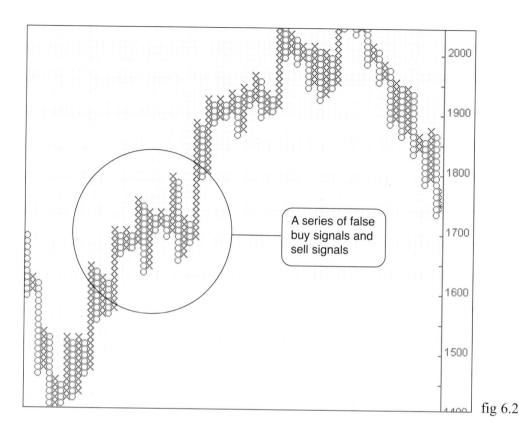

A series of false buy signals and sell signals

fig 6.2

Now consider the 10pt chart above which has a box size of closer to half of one percent.

Just like the 20pt chart, it signals the bottom very well. But as soon as the market gets to 1700 the 10pt chart disintegrates into a mess. It gives a repeat buy signal at 1710. It then reverses, giving a sell signal at 1660 which fails as it re-reverses and gives a fresh buy signal at 1750 which again works for a while (up to 1790), long enough to put a stop into place, but then reverses again to generate another sell signal, which again fails as the market re-reverses. Compare that fevered trading pattern to the serenity of the 20pt chart which has no sell signals of any kind at that point.

I find point & figure charts much more reliable the bigger the box size that is used. I use a box size of about 0.5% for the Dow (50 points), 0.8% to 1.2% for the FTSE (50 points), and box sizes of 1.2% to 2.5% for individual equities. That doesn't mean I don't look at the smaller size charts. I do, but the bigger box charts have primacy.

Test it yourself. Choose what's best for you. You'll see very quickly when looking at the same share with 2 different box sizes which chart portrays an orderly advance/decline and which chart is too inert/too demented. But as you'll see in Chapter 8, it has been proven that bigger box sizes produce more accurate charts.

Why do the funny X's and O's work?

When my first article on point & figure charts was published in the *Evening Standard*, the production team, who had been editing a business daily for years, were amazed. I guess they had never seen anything like it. Poking a little fun must have been irresistible. The article had a cartoon of a man looking at a noughts-and-crosses puzzle with a thought bubble saying "Ah, a buying opportunity!" and a sub-headline contained the piratical "X marks the spot". When I am sitting on a train updating my charts manually, I can see fellow travellers' necks craning as they look in stupefaction at the strangeness of the chart.

I have already explained the theory about why charts "work". I shall not repeat that to any great extent here. In essence, by employing a method of columnar reversals, the funny Xs and Os clearly demonstrate consolidation or broad equilibrium when the market is moving sideways. It is disequilibrium between the forces of supply and demand which produces sustained price movement and that too is portrayed very well by the point & figure chart.

Logically, it must be relevant to know why the price has broken out of a state of equilibrium. But very often one doesn't know, so the chartist trusts the price action. There are many occasions when the reason for a rise or fall in the market is not obvious at the time. It only becomes clearer much later. Eugene Ionesco, the French dramatist, observed rather drily that you can only predict things after they have happened.

Even when you do know why the breakout occurred, you often do not know how much weight to accord a certain factor, whether the market will agree with the weight you place on it, or how durable the factor will be. The chart takes that value judgment out of your hands, which is very useful, at least for me, because I do not have the time or the inclination to do detailed analysis of the world economy, corporate balance sheets or any other such sleep-inducing matters.

I still prefer my swing charts when it comes to calling the market as a whole, but I never fail to look at my point & figure charts, and when it comes to individual equities, point & figure is used with, and prevails over, the swing charts.

7 POINT & FIGURE SIGNALS

- Introduction

- The signals
  The Double Top and Double Bottom
  The Bullish Signal
  The Bearish Signal
  The Bearish Signal Reversed
  The Bullish Signal Reversed
  Triangles
  The Triple Top
  The Ascending Triple Top
  The Spread Triple Top
  The Triple Top with Long Tail
  The Bull Trap
  The Catapult
  The Triple Bottom
  The Descending Triple Bottom
  The Spread Triple Bottom
  The Triple Bottom with Long Tail
  The Long Tail Down
  The High Pole

- My evaluation

- My favourite point & figure signals
  The Triple Top with Rising Lows
  The Triple Bottom with Lower Highs
  The Bearish or Bullish Shakeout

- The Whipsaw

Introduction

Point & figure signals are so simple to understand that they require little explanation. Accordingly, in this chapter, I run briefly through the main signals, and I provide my personal evaluation thereafter. Then I deal in more depth with my two favourite point & figure signals.

If, after reading the first half of this chapter you still struggling to understand how point & figure signals work, please go to the free point & figure library at www.marcrivalland.com or buy one of the standard works on point & figure:

- *The Three-Point Reversal Method of Point & Figure Construction and Formations* by Michael L Burke (Chartcraft-1993)

- *Point & Figure Charting* by Thomas Dorsey (John Wiley & Sons 1995)

- *Point & Figure (Commodity and Stock Trading Techniques)* by Dr Kermit C Zieg (Traders Press 1997)

- *How to Use the 3-point Reversal Method of Point & Figure Stock Market Trading* by A.W. Cohen (Chartcraft Inc.1947) - currently out of print.

In many cases, I have illustrated the various chart patterns with examples from my columns in the *Evening Standard* and *Investors Chronicle*. I hope this is not too jarring. It is not meant to suggest that I am a whizzkid. I have done it because I thought it would be interesting and it would dispel any notion of 20/20 hindsight. It should also make clear that using point & figure charts is a relatively easy and disciplined way to trade the markets. Some of the calls I made in my columns did not work out. I would have included them here if I thought there was something significant to be learned from them.

The Double Top and Double Bottom

The most basic point & figure formations are the double top and double bottom.

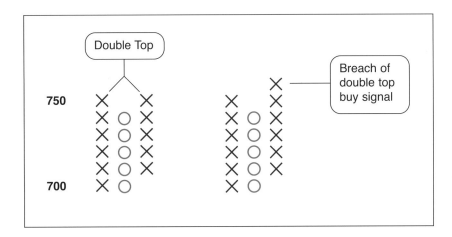

fig 7.1a

The first column of Xs depicts the stock advancing to 750p. At that point sellers temporarily overcame buyers and forced the stock back down to 700p, depicted by the column of Os. It could fairly be said that 750p was a point of resistance, a point where the force of the buying power was overcome. Thereafter the stock advances back up to 750p, forming a double top at that level. Until it breaches the established level of resistance, no safe conclusion could be drawn about the future destination of the stock. Once 760p prints, the dominance of the buyers is re-affirmed. The breach of the double top is said to constitute a buy signal. Note that in forming the double top at 750p, the stock may pause at that level for several days, or perhaps only a few minutes. It matters not.

The converse formation is the double bottom.

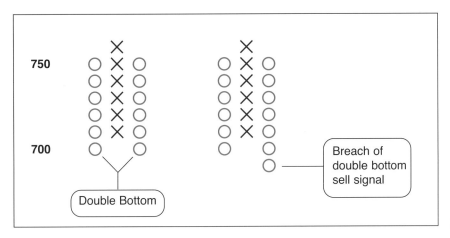

fig 7.1b

Although A.W. Cohen starts off with these two formations, in my opinion they are simply not reliable enough to count as buy/sell signals.

Naturally you will see a lot of double tops and bottoms being breached in the course of any trend. The breach of a double top in an uptrend is valuable in that the making of new highs confirms the continuation of the uptrend. By contrast when there is a breach of a double bottom during an uptrend, it is a negative sign. It casts doubt on the continuation of the uptrend because the presumed support (made by the first column of Os) has not held.

Of course, on a small box chart the support which has failed to hold may have been so minor that its breach is almost irrelevant. If you take the price action on a bar chart, and you examine it to see exactly what it takes to form a breach of double bottom you will notice that in no real sense can the market be described as having been in an equilibrium before the breach. I prefer signals that clearly portray a meaningful disequilibrium.

There are two good reasons, however, not to ignore double tops and bottoms:

1. Occasionally there is no clearer signal from any of my charts, including my swing charts, other than the breach of a double bottom in an uptrend, or the breach of a double top in a downtrend. Very occasionally I use that signal to close an unsatisfactory position.

2. It is worth looking out for the breach of a double bottom in an uptrend or the breach of a double top in a downtrend (i.e what looks like negative price action). These formations can convert themselves into one of my favourite signals, the bullish and bearish shakeout, by reversing shortly after the double top or bottom is breached.

The Bullish Signal

This point & figure formation is known as the bullish signal because it has the classic pattern of each rally making a higher high and each setback making a higher low. Although I like the series of rising lows, the bullish signal always makes me a little nervous because the buyers never seem to be winning comprehensively. Each rally only barely exceeds the high of the previous rally. What is really needed is some acceleration. Marks and Spencer had just started that acceleration phase when I reviewed it in the *Evening Standard* in early February 2001. It became the best performing FTSE 100 stock of 2001.

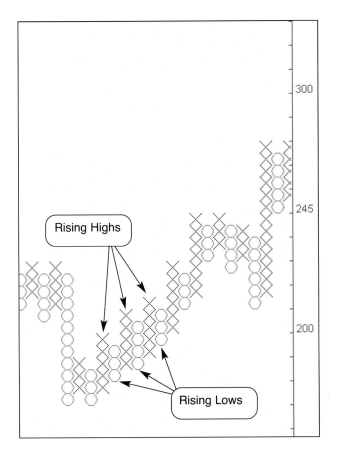

fig 7.2

The Bearish Signal

The bearish signal is the opposite of the bullish signal. The chart of Vodafone in the period June-August 2000 demonstrates this pattern.

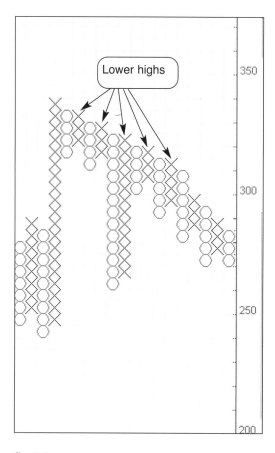

fig 7.3

The Bearish Signal Reversed

The succession of lower lows and lower highs in the bearish signal is classic bear market action. It suggests an evolving consensus that the stock is overpriced. You expect the force of selling which is producing persistently lower highs to complete a rout of the buyers at some point. But when the bearish signal suddenly reverses, it has all the hallmarks of a bear squeeze. Whatever the reason, A.W. Cohen found this to be one of the most reliable point & figure chart formations. I don't dissent. It is a reliable formation although somewhat rare. A properly constituted bearish signal reversed has at least 7 columns.

In the chart below of the FTSE transport index, the events of September 11th initially produced a rout, but there came a time when, although eager selling was producing lower highs, the buyers were no longer being routed. Eventually the sellers were overcome. The buy signal occurs the first time a prior high is breached.

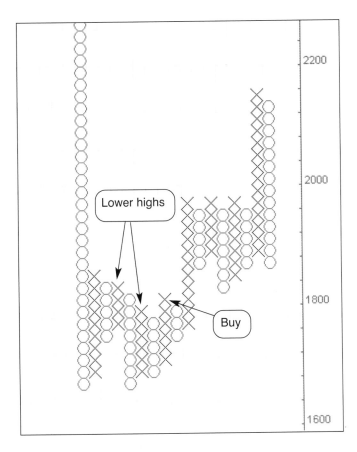

fig 7.4

The Bullish Signal Reversed

The market is lulled into a false sense of security by the succession of rising lows and highs which occurs in the bullish signal. When that sequence is interrupted by a breach of the previous lows it can set off liquidation which feeds on itself driving prices substantially lower. Shell in the early part of 2001 provides a good example.

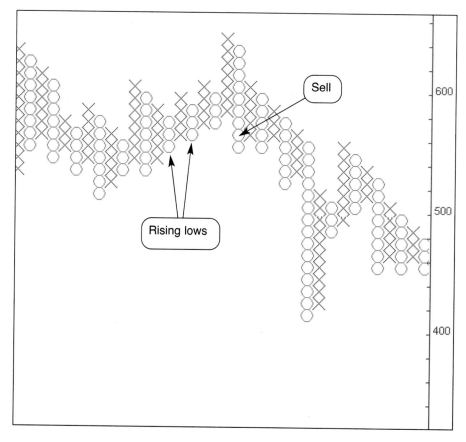

fig 7.5

Triangles

The symmetrical triangle usually has at least 5 columns. Its development is often a sign of the market waiting for some important news like the outcome of a Fed meeting, or annual results. The sellers become more reluctant to push the market down to its old lows and the buyers become more reluctant to push the market up to its old highs. Volume often diminishes. Then the news breaks. There is usually a swift move.

I don't trust the triangle. In my opinion, it is the most treacherous of the point & figure signals. I have the impression that the whole market is aware that the index or share is winding itself into an ever tighter coil. When the news comes for which the market has been waiting, there is often a knee-jerk reaction which sends the market speeding away from the apex of the triangle, only for second thoughts to prevail, whereupon the market rushes all the way back up to the apex and sometimes beyond. There are fewer treacherous triangles on charts which have bigger box values i.e. more than 1.5%.

But a good example of a triangle formation producing good profits was BP in early 1999. The first triangle is a classic, and note that there were two more irregular triangles thereafter.

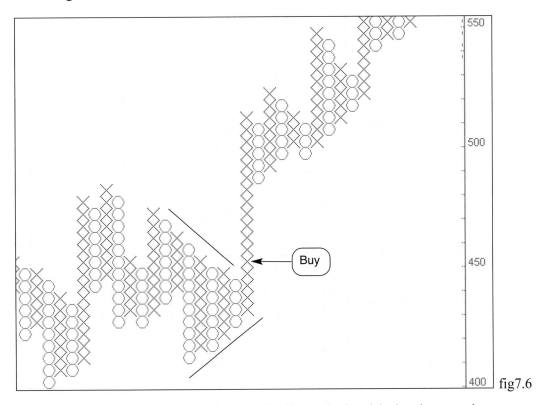

fig7.6

The upper edge of the triangle is of course similar to the bearish signal reversed.

An example of a triangle leading traders astray was EMAP in February 2002.

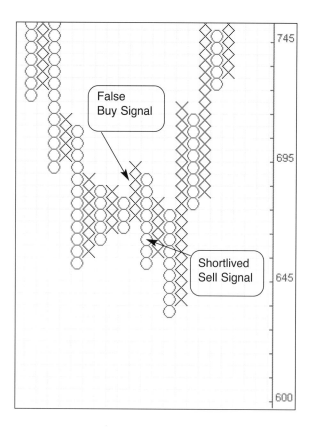

fig 7.7

The triangle first produced an upward breakout, which immediately reversed, no doubt causing traders to operate a stop loss and perhaps to go short, only for the share price to reverse once again a few days later.

In A.W. Cohen's book, the bullish triangle (one which breaks upwards) has the lowest percentage profitability of all, and the bearish triangle (one which breaks downwards) has the fourth lowest percentage profitability of all. The profitability figures used in Cohen's book still suggest that the triangle is a worthwhile formation, but I'm still wary of them. Perhaps it's not too important. They are rare formations. They occur about 2% of the time according to Robert Earl Davis's study.

The Triple Top

This formation and its variations are very important. When the market is repelled twice at the same level it is plain that a level of resistance is established. When it breaks through the resistance on a third (or fourth or subsequent) occasion, you could not wish for a clearer demonstration of disequilibrium. The clothing group Next gave a fine buy signal in May 2000.

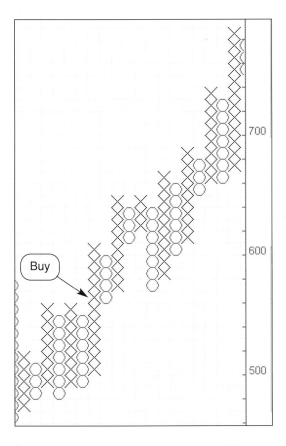

fig 7.8

Michael Burke is of the view that whilst triple tops used to be the strongest buy signals during the period 1950-1970, they can't now be said to be any better than double tops. I must confess that is not my experience. I'm still very happy with this formation.

The Ascending Triple Top

The second rally is repelled at a slightly higher point than the first. On the third (or subsequent) occasion, the sellers are overcome. Two examples of the ascending triple top are seen in the chart of BSkyB. In the first example, the upward run was cut short by the 11th September tragedy, but after regrouping BSkyB repeated the formation to continue its run. This second signal lead me to recommend a swing trade in the shares in *Investors Chronicle* of 19th October 2001.

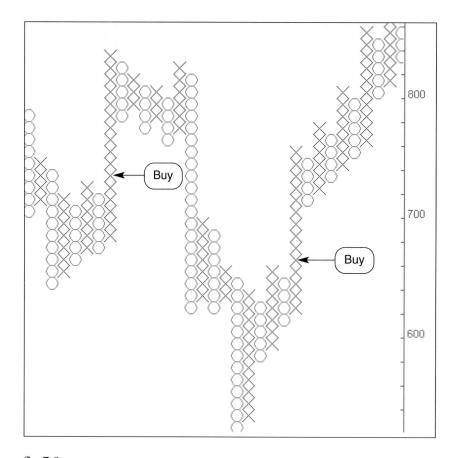

fig 7.9

The Spread Triple Top

The name speaks for itself. The points of resistance are spread out, not tightly bunched together.

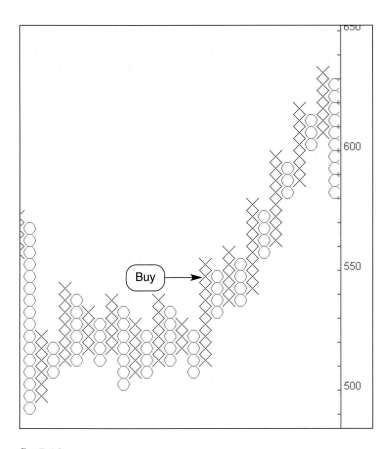

fig 7.10

Look at the base which BP formed between 500p and 535p. The disequilibrium which occurs when the price trades at 545p is as obvious as it could be, which is why I suggested in *Investors Chronicle* of 11th January 2002 that readers should buy at that price.

The Triple Top with Long Tail

A.W. Cohen said that the existence of a long tail causes the move to be particularly dynamic when the triple top is breached. I agree, provided that it is understood that I am referring to a short-term move.

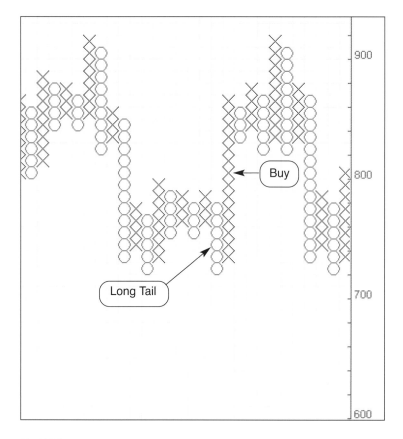

fig 7.11

The reason for this dynamism is probably that the formation has some resemblance to a trap. Bears are being squeezed as a perceived downtrend fails to emerge after the earlier breach of a triple bottom.

The Bull Trap

Michael Burke attributes this formation to the huge popularity of triple tops. Effectively, the chartist is paying a penalty for his buying point being known well in advance. The share price breaches a triple top by one box but there is no follow-through buying. The share price advances no further. Indeed, sellers, who may have been waiting on the sidelines for the chart-based buying to come in, start driving down prices. It is a bull trap. The share then executes a 3 box reversal. The assumed disequilbrium was an illusion.

It is important to note that Michael Burke regards it as a sell signal once the 3 box reversal is executed because there will be a number of bulls trapped who will be forced to liquidate.

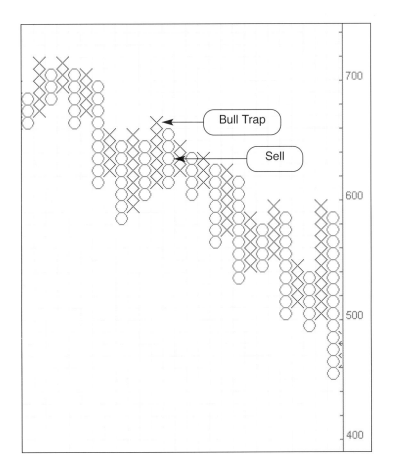

fig 7.12

A good example is provided by Diageo in September 1999. The bullish looking triple top breakout was a trap, and if traders had regarded it not simply as a failed buy signal but also as a sell signal when the shares made a 3 box reversal, they would have made back their losses and more. But I don't like trading this formation much. It is difficult to distinguish from the catapult.

The Catapult

The catapult, in contrast to the bull trap, is a bullish formation, which means that its similarity to and potential confusion with the bull trap is most unhelpful. A.W. Cohen was of the view that this formation occurred about 50% of the time after a triple top breakout. That statistic is probably not true of today's markets. Just like the bull trap, the market breaches a triple top and then has a pullback. The breach may advance by between 1 and 3 boxes, usually (although A.W. Cohen says up to 7 boxes). There is then a pullback, usually into the base from which the share has just broken out. In other words, it looks just like the bull trap at that point. In the past I have tried to distinguish between the two by calling a formation a bull trap if the share advances just one box and reverses, and by assuming that it is a catapult if it advances 2 or more boxes before pulling back. Unfortunately that distinction doesn't always work. I've seen bull traps that have advanced 2 boxes and catapults which have started after 1 box.

It's all a bit muddled and a recipe for losing money so it seems to me. Look at the chart on the next page of NASDAQ before it made its final break to the 2001 lows.

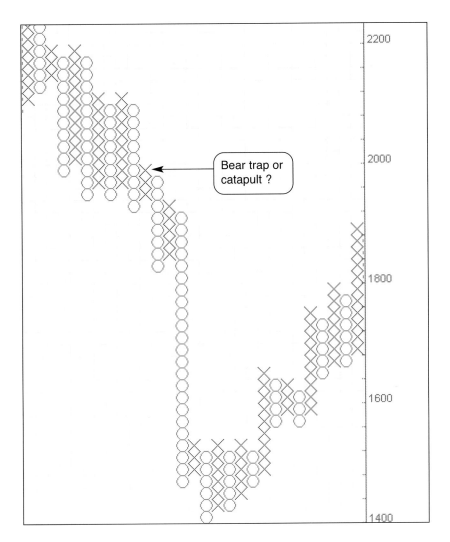

fig 7.13

This was a classic breach of a triple bottom, immediately followed by a 3 box reversal. You would have been a little annoyed to have bought it at that point, reading it as a bear trap. On the other hand it would have cost you only 4 boxes because a stop loss would have taken you short again when the formation proved to be a catapult.

In general, I attach no weight to the 3 box reversal at this point. Since it could be either a bear trap (bullish) or a bearish catapult (bearish), I make no assumptions and I let the market unfold. Eventually it tells me.

The Triple Bottom

After this sell signal at 600p was noted in the *Evening Standard* of July 2001, Enterprise Oil formed another base at the lower level of 570p to 610p before declining to 460p.

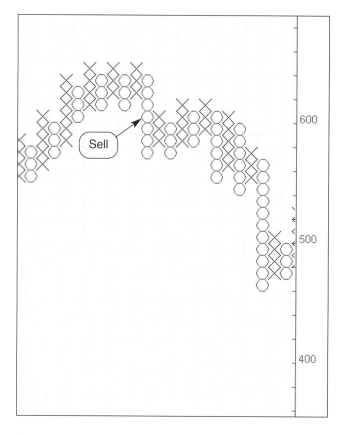

fig 7.14

The Descending Triple Bottom

The sell signal given by Rio Tinto on 11th June 2001 was a fine example of the descending triple bottom. Note the early similarity between the descending triple bottom and the bearish signal. The difference is the downward acceleration in the former pattern and the absence of it in the latter.

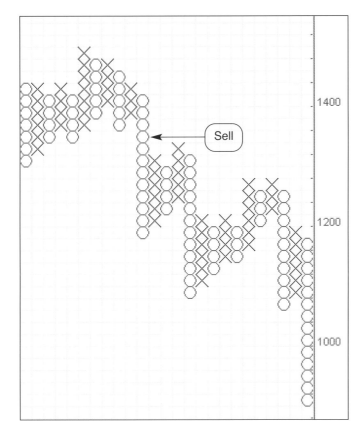

fig 7.15

The Spread Triple Bottom

After this spread triple bottom sell signal in February 2001 at 1240p, noted in the *Evening Standard*, Shire declined quickly to 840p before staging a recovery. I made the point in Chapter 2 about markets falling much faster than they rise. You won't be surprised to learn that I like the triple bottom and its variations.

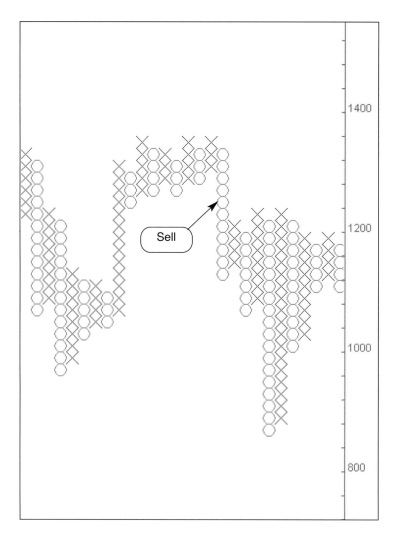

fig 7.16

The Triple Bottom with Long Tail

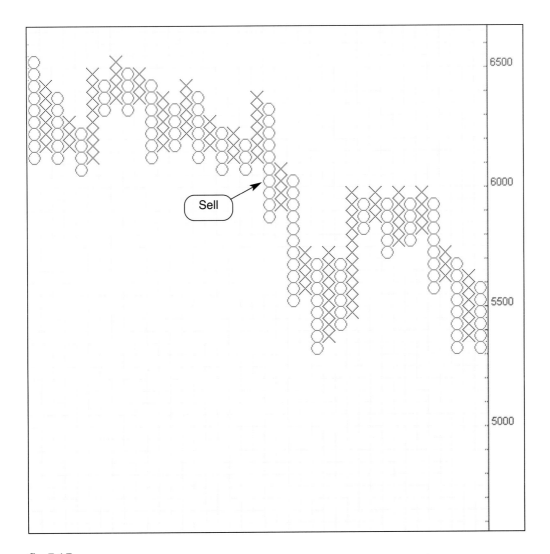

fig 7.17

The short-term dynamism of the long tail is well illustrated here. After the FTSE gave its triple bottom sell signal on 20 February 2001, the market fell over 700 points in 22 trading days.

The Long Tail Down

This occurs when a share has an unusually long or unusually steep fall without any of the minor rallies which one typically sees. Tom Dorsey says that the share must fall about 20 boxes (units of price movement). The buy signal occurs on the first 3 box reversal. I must say I have never been convinced that this is a safe chart formation. I don't see how it portrays an enduring alteration in the equilibrium between buyers and sellers in favour of the buyers. To me it simply represents a highly risky form of bottom fishing. It works on the supposition that the first rally will be the start of an durable upward move, or at any rate a profitable bounce, which seems a dangerous stance.

However, I have to report that it did in fact work (!) with Kingfisher in October 2000.

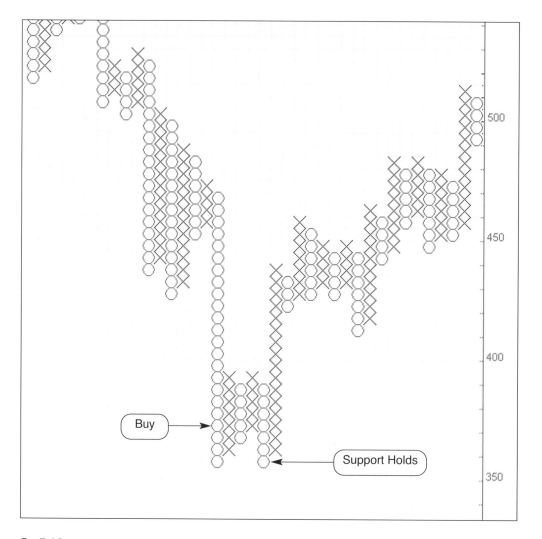

fig 7.18

Tom Dorsey wisely advises operating a stop loss immediately if the buy signal fails and the market makes a lower low. He also makes a convincing case for not using the long tail up as a sell signal. But whilst I consider this formation too dangerous for swing traders to use, it can be used, in conjunction with options, by long-term buy and hold investors, as I explain in Chapter 11.

Michael Burke also uses a variation of the long tail down (or up) principle in his analysis of bullish percent charts which are a composite of the number of bullish charts in a sector or market. Since there is an underlying change in equilibrium in this respect, one can see the force of using the principle with such charts.

The High Pole

Earl Blumenthal, another famous point & figure chartist, developed this signal. The pattern is formed when a column of Xs exceeds the previous column of Xs by at least 3Xs and then gives up more than half of its total gains in the next column of Os. This is less of an actual sell signal than a warning signal. I do not pay much attention to it when the trend is up, but in a downtrend it can be very effective in picking up bear market rallies on the point or during the course of failure, as the chart below of Standard Chartered demonstrates. The first high pole in November 1999 occurs in the middle of an uptrend and can't really be considered a success, but the next high pole, also in an uptrend, is successful, as are the three which occur in a downtrend in the early months of 2000. With minor variations, signals 3, 4 and 5 below represented Earl Blumenthal's favourite signal to sell short.

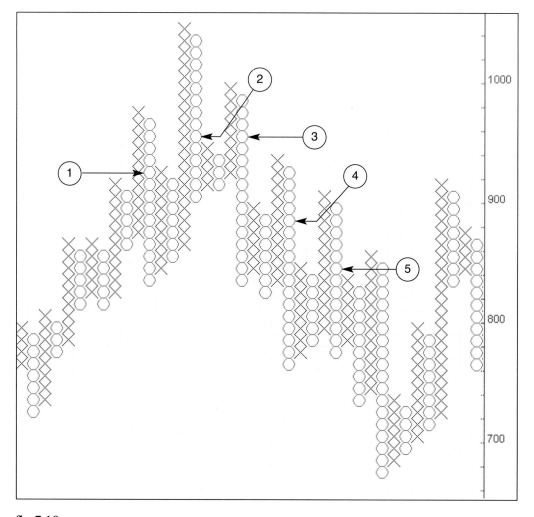

fig 7.19

Another superb example of the high pole in a bear market was the NASDAQ Comp in April 2002.

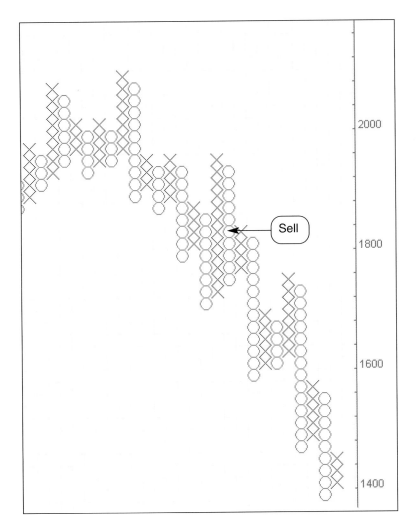

fig 7.20

Count the number of Xs in the substantial bear market rally from late February to 12th March 2002. It was 12. The sell signal occurs on the sixth O (1820), at which point the market has given up 7 out of the 12 Xs. Thereafter the NASDAQ plunges to new lows for the year.

121

My evaluation

I deal with the reliability of point & figure charting as a whole in Chapter 8. So far as I am aware there has only been one study into the reliability of individual point & figure patterns. It was done by Professor Robert Earl Davis, and the results for each signal are published in A.W. Cohen's original book as well as in the books by Kermit Zieg and Tom Dorsey noted at the beginning of this chapter. Not all the above signals were studied by Davis - those such as the high pole and long tail down were not considered. The study covered the period 1954-1964, apart from two stocks which were analysed from 1914 to 1964. It was found, for example, that during a bull market, with proper use of trend lines and price objectives, the triple top formation would be profitable 87.9% of the time for an average gain of 28.7% over 6.8 months. It was unprofitable 12.1% of the time for an average loss of 8.3% over 2.2 months. All of the formations examined had reliability rates of at least 80% except the bullish triangle which had a reliability rate of 71%. These reliability rates are simply unachievable in today's markets. It would be a license to print a money. This is my personal opinion, but look at the charts and they will prove it to you. The more recent work by Dr Kermit Zieg also proves the point.

My opinion of the individual point & figure formations is as follows:

Double top/Double bottom

It is not worth trading this signal, on the whole. It simply describes a single countertrend rally or dip, which may have lasted just one day, before the trend continues. If you think you can make money trading such minor corrections, it may be the signal for you. Good luck.

Bullish signal/ Bearish signal

Usually you don't have to consider this signal, it is so rare. If it only has 3 columns, then it is effectively just a double top or double bottom with a rising low/falling high. You'd best advised to ignore it. If it has 5 columns or more, it is broadly indistinguishable from an ascending triple top formation/descending triple bottom formation, and as such it is reliable.

Bullish Signal reversed/Bearish Signal reversed

They are reliable formations because they usually describe a squeeze of the bears or panic liquidation by the bulls. But as buy/sell signals they are often shortlived, either because the panic subsides or because a new equilibrium forms from which a fresh point & figure signal is generated.

Triangles

The most treacherous of all. You need to be a day trader, watching the price action like a hawk to see if this formation is going to turn against you. Don't trust it.

Triple Top/Triple Bottom and their variations

These are good reliable signals, harmed only by their visibility. Michael Burke says these signals have become so popular that they have spawned the bull and bear trap because everyone knows where the chartists will be buying. I'm sure he's right in some circumstances, but I still find these formations reliable, particularly the triple bottom and its variations.

Bull Trap/Bear Trap

You do see them, but they are very risky to trade on charts with a small box value (less than 1.5%). They are a bit better on charts with big box values. Effectively you are relying on the possibility that the breach of important resistance, and a failure to follow through, means that a trap has been sprung. It can and does happen that way, but bear in mind no important support has been breached. This formation can easily convert itself into the catapult. I never trade this formation.

Catapult

Effectively this is a triple top or bottom which hints at a bull trap but then moves in the direction of the initial break. I don't regard it as a separate formation. I think of it as variation of the triple top/bottom.

Long Tail Down

A highly risky form of bottom-fishing, but since you are only ever risking 4 boxes, the risk/reward ratio is not bad.

High Pole/Low Pole

A high pole in an uptrend is only a warning signal, and it is one that I don't pay that much attention to. A high pole in a downtrend was Earl Blumenthal's favourite signal to go short. I too like it, but there is no really good place to put a stop loss, so the risk/reward ratio is poor. If I see a high pole in a downtrend, I revert to my swing charts to see if they will give me a reasonably close place to put a stop loss. A low pole in a downtrend is a warning signal. A low pole in an uptrend doesn't seem to have the same sort of significance as the high pole in a downtrend. I keep an eye on it, but I seldom trade it.

My favourite point & figure signals

The Triple Top with Rising Lows

There are multiple examples of the triple top with rising lows yielding fine moves. The post-September 11th low in the NASDAQ (see page 93) was a classic. Another fine example is ARM in August 2000. The rising lows are a clear sign of increasing eagerness on the part of buyers.

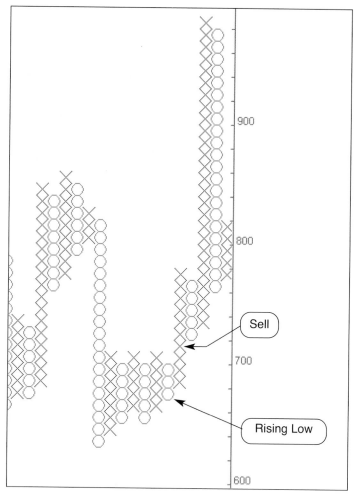

fig 7.21

Obviously this signal, like any other, provides no guarantees. By October 2002 Vodafone was in a bear market. This time the signal led nowhere, although the price action did give you enough time to raise a stop to a level where losses were minimal.

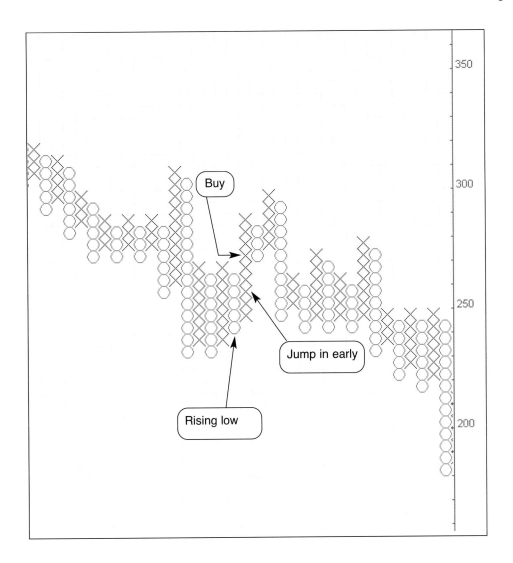

fig 7.22

What about leaping into the market before the breach of the triple top has been completed? Is there mileage in jumping the gun by buying on the first 3 box reversal to the upside, as soon as you can see that a higher low has been made, instead of waiting for the breakout from the triple top?

Logically one shouldn't because the market is still in a broad state of equilibrium. But I do occasionally jump in early in certain limited circumstances:

1. There must be a reasonable advantage to be gained. There was no point in jumping in early in the ARM chart above. You'd be buying right up against the resistance. All you needed to do was wait for the market to advance one more box. It follows that I only consider jumping in early when the base is deep i.e. the columns are long. The Vodafone chart just satisfies the minimum criterion. There are 3 boxes to be gained by jumping in early.

2. I want the shape of the formation, if it fails, and if it proves to have been a mistake to jump in early, to resemble the bullish signal reversed. In the Vodafone chart, this would have been the case. In other words, had Vodafone executed another 3 box reversal to the down side, there would have been a sell signal upon which I could have acted to recover the loss from jumping in early. The chart below shows what I mean.

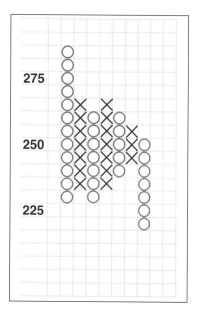

fig 7.23

In February 2002 Reuters executed exactly this formation.

3. Other considerations apply. It didn't matter what the shape was in late September 2001, I was not going to sell the NASDAQ. It had already had a calamitous sell-off. Oversold readings were extreme. I was simply waiting for the market to settle and give a proper buy signal. So no jumping in early, and no selling if the triple top buy signal failed.

The Triple Bottom with Lower Highs

The chart below shows the Royal and Sun Alliance coming off its all time highs in April 1998, the breach of the triple bottom beautifully preceded by the lower high. The lower high is a clear sign of increasing eagerness on the part of sellers. It may be that existing holders of the stock have grown more gloomy or short sellers have become more aggressive. In the case of triple bottoms I never jump in early - markets seem to pause often when going up, without the pauses having any wider significance.

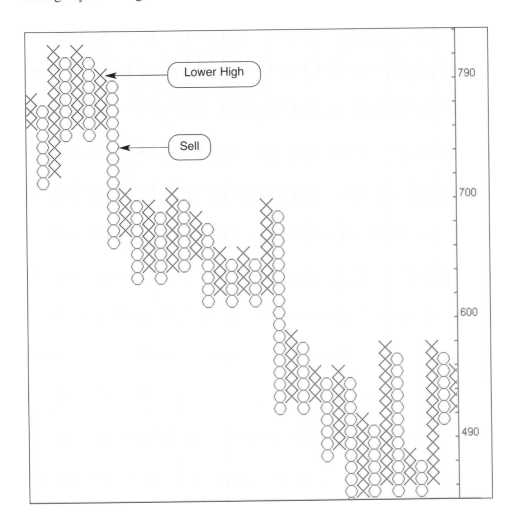

fig 7.24

The Bearish or Bullish Shakeout

The shakeout formation was first identified by Earl Blumenthal. In his book published in 1993 Michael Burke thought it to be the best point & figure formation of recent years.

The heart of the bullish shakeout signal is a decline by a share or index which breaches a double bottom. Traditionally that has been regarded as a negative development, and as the bulls perceive that support in the market has not held, liquidation takes place. Other traders may enter short positions. But if the market makes a 3 box reversal within a box or two of breaching the double bottom and then reverses, it is often a trap. In fact, Earl Blumenthal's hypothesis was that the first sell signal in a bull market is actually a buy signal!

In this formation, like the bull trap, the buy signal occurs on the first 3 box reversal. In most other point & figure formations the buy signal comes only after a consolidation phase has ended in a breakout. The chart of Six Continents in October 1992 shows this formation clearly.

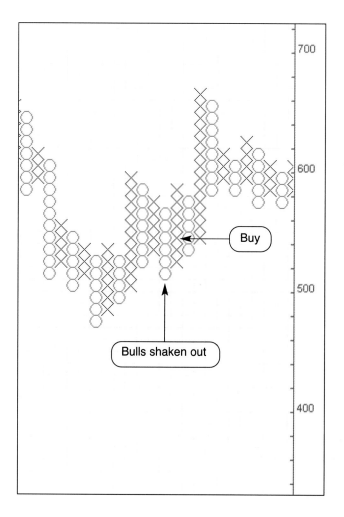

fig 7.25

Michael Burke has a number of other criteria for the establishment of this signal which I do not follow, so I suppose my shakeout is a really a variation on the original.

My criteria for the bullish shakeout are:

1. The previous signal given by the share must have been a bullish one.

2. As the market declines, a double bottom is breached by 1 box or 2 boxes (if the box value is high) but no more than 3 boxes (if the box value is not high).

3. The market then executes an upward 3 box reversal. BUY and place a stop and reverse below the lows i.e 4 boxes away.

What I like about this formation is that it gives one a *double option*. Do you see what would happen if no trap results - if the breach of the double bottom really was an early signal of coming weakness? The chart pattern would convert itself into a descending triple bottom.

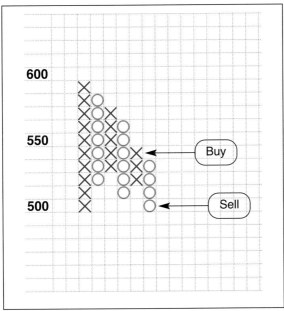

fig 7.26

It follows that one has the market surrounded. Either the shakeout will prove to be a profitable buy signal, or a descending triple bottom sell signal will be given which itself should be profitable. Of course it is possible that the shakeout signal will cause a loss, and the descending triple bottom will cause a loss as well, but that is very, very rare.

The very best feature of this formation is that the initial risk is only ever 4 boxes because one is buying on the first 3 box reversal, and placing a stop and reverse order to capture the descending triple bottom.

The converse formation is the **bearish shakeout**. Look at Vodafone in 2002.

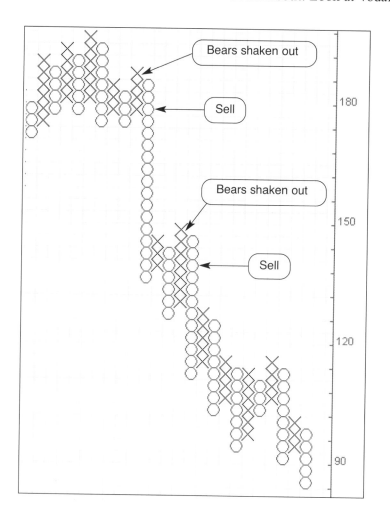

fig 7.27

The first sell signal at 177p was not countermanded at any point before the lows at 93p. The same is true of the second sell signal at 141p.

But the shakeout does often fizzle out after a relatively short period so you would need a rule such as the raising of a stop loss to your entry point to prevent losses from offsetting these 2 sparkling profits.

The bullish and bearish shakeouts have a high level of accuracy, particularly if measured over a short period. It is the closest I come to day trading. My usual objective on the shakeout is a mere 5 to 7 boxes which usually takes no time at all to happen. Likewise my objective on the descending triple bottom is modest.

Take the Dow Jones index 50pt chart from the start of 1997 as an example:

fig 7.28

I am looking at this chart mechanically which is not the real position as I would always be considering the swing chart as well. Imagine one sets a profit objective of 6 boxes for these purposes. That may sound very little, but on the Dow it is 300 points which is not bad.

1. A bullish shakeout in January 1997. There is easily 300 points profit available, especially after the formation converts itself into a spread triple top.

2. Another bullish shakeout in March 1997. It resolves to the downside by converting itself into a descending triple bottom. The initial loss of 200 points is offset by a profit of 300 points.

3. Another bullish shakeout in June 1997 yields 300 points.

4. Another bullish shakeout in October 1997 converts into a descending triple bottom sell signal. The initial loss of 200 points is offset by a profit of 300 points.

5. A bearish shakeout in November 1997 works to begin with, travelling 200 points in the right direction before a second reversal leads to a strong rally. The initial loss of 200 points is offset by a profit of 300 points.

6. A bullish shakeout in April 1998 leads nowhere and after building a base, the Dow falls through a bullish signal reversed triggering a clear sell signal, coincidentally at one's entry point. Scratch trade.

7. A bearish shakeout in June 1998 leads to a profit of 300 points.

8. I don't count this as a bearish shakeout. It is too equivocal. It could also be a bearish signal reversed. Disappointment at missing the 1300 point move is assuaged by the knowledge that the high of this equivocal signal happened to be the third day on the swing chart in the middle of the 1998 linear phase, so the move would not have been missed.

9. A bearish shakeout in September 1998 yields 300 points profit.

You may sniff at this sort of performance, but I believe the point is well made that this formation is highly reliable. There are 7 profits and one scratch trade. The Vodafone 3p box chart during the period January 2001 to May 2002 likewise produced 1 scratch trade and 7 profits using a profit target of 5 boxes and raising the stop loss to the entry point once the share had advanced 4 boxes in the right direction.

Because of its reliability, the shakeout provides me with the *one qualification* to my strategy that swing charts rule when timing the market as a whole. Shakeout formations sometimes occur when the swing chart gives a change in trend signal, which turns out to be false or leads nowhere. It is a useful filter to be looking at the point & figure chart, alive to possibility of a shakeout. If the point & figure chart signals a shakeout, I always pay heed to it, even if the same story is not being told by the swing chart.

The Whipsaw

As I've mentioned, although one has the market surrounded, it can happen that the shakeout's double option is simply the occasion for two helpings of losses, which is happily rare. The chart of Rio Tinto in 1999 provides an example:

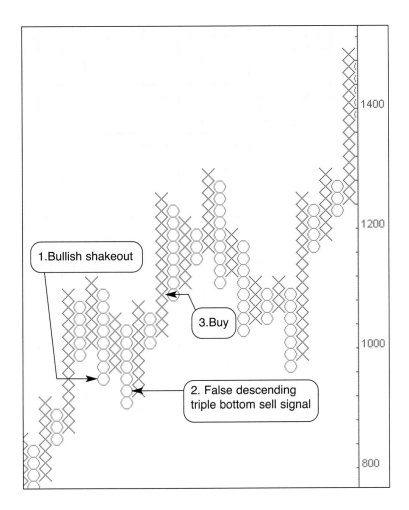

fig 7.29

1. Rio Tinto shakes out the bulls by making a lower low on 13th May then reverses upwards and gives a buy signal on 18th May.

2. After some progress, the share reverses and triggers a descending triple bottom sell signal on 26th May but that signal too turns out to be false.

3. Happily an ascending triple top with rising lows develops. The inference is that buyers can scarcely contain their enthusiasm, until somewhat later in the year, they are sedated by a dose of reality (as Warren Buffett puts it).

8 POINT & FIGURE TACTICS

- Choose the right security

- When to take profits

- Don't trade every chart formation you see

- Reliability of point & figure charts

- Tailpiece 1

- Tailpiece 2

Choose the Right Security

Allied Domecq is one of the biggest companies in Britain and yet look how one would have struggled trying to trade this stock with a point & figure chart.

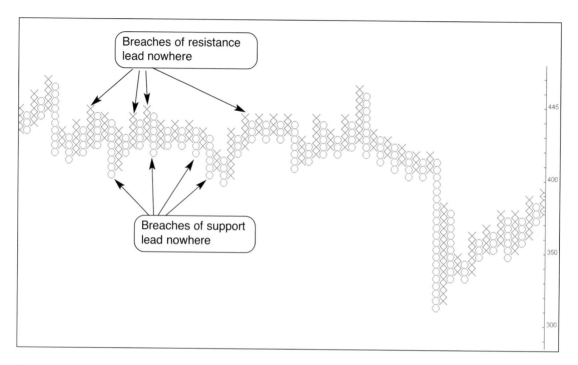

fig 8.1

And that struggle does not apply only to charts which show a long trading range. There are other stocks, most of them with low volatility, which lumber on steadily. Every now and then they experience a bout of skittishness and they have a mini-sell off. That sell off breaches a support level on the chart, generating a sell signal, which turns out to be a trap, or at least a dead end, when investors nerves settle. These stocks may represent excellent investments for buy and hold armchair investors, but they are murder for a swing trader.

I don't mean to suggest that every old economy stock is unsuitable for swing trading. Far from it. But as I've noted before, check the chart to see whether your trading tactics would have had any success in the past.

Some might have thought that the volatile NASDAQ Composite would not be the ideal market to plot on a point and figure chart. But look at fig 8.2 opposite to see how beautifully it works. I start just after the peak at 5000. Millions of people lost money on this downswing (including my self-select pension fund), but swing traders using charts should have cleaned up.

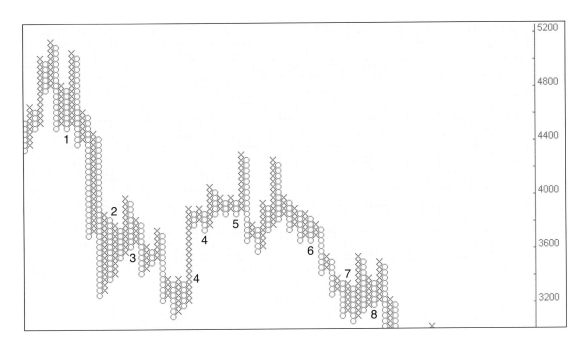

fig 8.2

I make plain that I traded bits of this downtrend rather than all of it, so part of the commentary below is plainly tainted by hindsight. But I suggest that I am sticking to the principles of the last 2 chapters. I start off first with the 40pt chart.

1. A triple bottom sell signal is given at 4320, after which the market falls 640 points in the first instance, a fall big enough to realize half or full profits. There is then a scary rally all the way up to the original sell signal and another slump.

2. An irregular triangle forms and a buy signal is generated at 3840. Because it's the treacherous triangle, one would have had no difficulty raising a stop to minimize losses once the market had advanced 4 further boxes to 4000. The stop is triggered as the market fails.

3. A bullish signal reversed sell signal/further irregular triangle sell signal occurs at 3560. Because of the triangular shape, it's probably not worth trading (it did in fact yield a small profit).

4. A classic triple top buy signal with rising lows occurs at 3400, and it is followed by a bullish shakeout buy signal and another triple top taking the market all the way to 4280, a 26% rise in 2 months.

5. A quadruple bottom sell signals occurs at 3800 which worked for a while but would probably have resulted in a small loss in the end.

6.   The secondary high in September is not well signalled at first, but later a very clear bearish signal develops with a sell signal at 3680 followed by a triple bottom sell signal at 3600 (the easier trade) which takes the market all the way down to 3040, ample room to take half or full profits.

7.   The NASDAQ makes another attempt at a rally with a bearish signal reversed buy signal at 3360 but after a move up to 3520 this breaks down. Probably a small loss here.

8.   A bullish signal reversed sell signal at 3120. As the market falls through 3000, switch charts to the 25pt chart. A steep rally probably stops one out at entry point and as a result you probably miss the next 800 points down. I know I did.

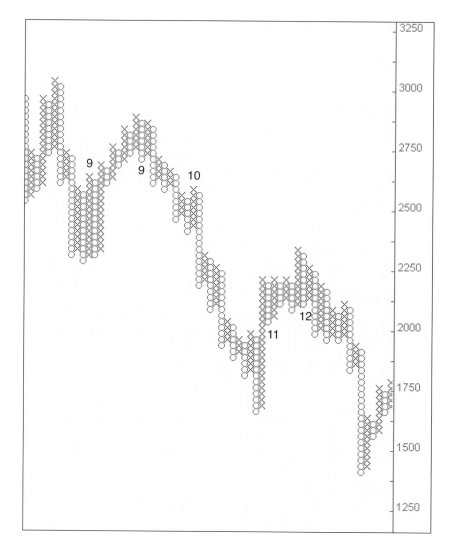

fig 8.3

9. An ascending triple top buy signal at 2675 evolves slowly and successfully taking the market up to 2875 before breaking down at 2700 with one of my favourite signals, this time the bearish version, the descending triple bottom with falling highs. Sell short.

10. A repeat sell signal is given with a bearish shakeout at 2500. The market falls away, in an orderly fashion, to 1650, a fall of 39% from the original sell signal at 2700.

11. Because the market has fallen through 2000, I am looking at both the 20pt and 25pt charts. After another bearish shakeout, the 25pt chart generates an ascending triple top buy signal at 1975 which takes the NASDAQ up to 2325 (gain 17.7%).

12. A bullish signal reversed with the shape of a triangle describes itself on the 25pt chart. Confirmed on the 20pt chart which has a very clear triangle. Don't touch. Sure enough the market plunges and instantly recovers.

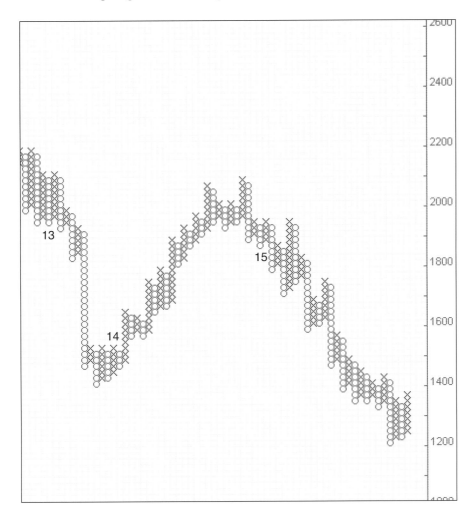

fig 8.4

13.   The 20pt chart gives a triple bottom sell signal at 1920, after which there is an immediate 3 box reversal. Is this the catapult or a bear trap? The 25pt chart says no bear trap. Stay short. The NASDAQ plunges to lows at 1400, a move of 27%.

14.   That triple top buy signal, again! The move starts at 1540 and goes all the way up to 2080, a move of 35% with several repeat buy signals on the way.

15.   A bullish signal reversed sell signal at 1920 suggests that the uptrend is over. It is followed by a descending triple bottom sell signal, and then a high pole in a downtrend sell signal.

I have not attempted to describe here a full trading strategy, but is this not a wonderful illustration of the effectiveness of point & figure charts?

When to take profits

Price objectives

A.W. Cohen put forward a system of vertical counts and horizontal counts to set a price target. The horizontal count measures the length of the base from which the market has broken out, i.e. the number of columns of Xs and Os, multiplies that by 3 and adds the product to the lowest point of the base to arrive at a price target.

Certainly as a matter of practice, one does often see a loose correlation between length of the base formation and extent of the ultimate move. But in my view, it is all a little tenuous. It is plain from Cohen's book that even he regards these as rather rudimentary tools. If you use modern software, it has the facility to measure the counts for you, and you can decide for yourself whether they are sufficiently reliable.

I don't use horizontal or vertical counts or indeed any mechanical method for setting price objectives.

Freewheeling approach

It is widely recognised that a buy signal in a chart will often last a few weeks or less. The fact that disequilibrium has occurred gives one no real insight into when and where the next equilibrium will be formed. Of course, the trader is hoping that it takes a big move for supply and demand to come back into balance, but it needn't be so. It can and does happen that the new equilibrium is found just fractionally above or below the old equilibrium.

The truth is that I don't have a rulebook when it comes to taking profits. That may be disappointing, but I don't pretend to know all the answers. My approach to taking profits is a more freewheeling, open knit approach.

Sometimes I wait for the point & figure chart to give me a sell signal. Other times, I set an arbitrary price target. One of the tools I use is the RSI - discussed in Chapter 10.

I am particularly keen on taking half profits quite promptly, which means the remaining half position can be run for free, as it were.

I am not alone in this. Tom Dorsey, avowedly not a short-term trader, thinks it wise even for investors to book part of their profits at an arbitrary level after a good advance.

Since swing trading usually involves holding a leveraged position (although it need not), any time that I have a profit of over 10% in an individual equity in just a few weeks, I am ready to hear the sound of the till at the first sign that a market move is running out of steam. My profit targets tend to be modest. I will usually bag as little as 9-10% half profits and then run the remaining half position. Once that reaches the stage of yielding a profit of 11-18%, I am ready to take full profits unless a (previously unperceived) linear phase is unfolding, or some other convincing reason presents itself for holding on, which usually doesn't happen.

With equity indices, I'm guided more by the swing chart. I've dealt with profit targets in Chapter 5.

Wall Street legend Bernard Baruch said you should always sell a stock so the person who buys it makes a profit. He also said "I made my money by selling too soon". I'm in Baruch's camp.

Don't trade every chart formation you see

Trading with the trend

Look at any point & figure chart and you will see a host of good signals. You will also see a number of buy or sell signals which start off well, but then reverse. This is typical. All that disequilibrium suggests is that the market will move in an unstable way until a new consensus is formed.

One of the most difficult aspects of point and figure charting is as follows: The chart gives a good buy signal and the share price moves up say 10 boxes (or units of value) from the base from which it has broken out. It then forms a new base. Then it breaks down. Should one sell, and if not, why not? Should one conclude that this is the end of an uptrend? What happens with a point & figure chart is that one seldom gets a long and sustained run without some worryingly negative chart pattern developing. Because the swing trader is usually leveraged, he cannot ignore adverse chart signals.

Are trend lines the solution?

The answer to this problem, according to A.W. Cohen, was not to trade against the trend. Very sound advice. Michael Burke makes the matter crystal clear by declining to call the sell signal a sell signal if it occurs in an uptrend. He re-christens it a "down" signal.

But what is the trend? A.W. Cohen's answer was to draw a trend line. Not the trend line that you frequently see some people draw connecting a series of bottoms or tops but simply a mechanical 45° trend line from the lowest point made by a stock which had just given a buy signal (vice versa for sell signals). As long as a stock remained above the 45° line it was considered to be in an uptrend and any sell signal which occurred was to be ignored.

You may think that a 45° line is a rather clunky, unsophisticated approach to defining a trend. Look at www.stockcharts.com and you will see just how often a share breaks its uptrend line (called the bullish support line) or its downtrend line (called the bearish resistance line) without that break actually signalling any change in trend.

The situation is not improved by drawing trend lines connecting highs or lows made in the past. Personally I am doubtful about this technique. Suppose a high were made 2 years ago, and then another intermediate lower high 1 year ago and then a further lower intermediate high 4 months ago. Many people will take a ruler and connect the 3 highs and declare that the market is in a downtrend until that trend line is broken. Let us say the trend line declines from left to right at a gradient of 31°. Why is the market not in a bear trend if it stops going down at the rate of 31°?

The only conclusion one should draw is that the momentum has changed, that the *rate* of decline has altered, not the propensity to decline. A breach of the trend line would not, logically, signal a new uptrend, or even the end of the old downtrend. In the fullness of time, the change in momentum may have relevant implications for the future trend, but that is a separate point. Nothing lasts forever.

I don't seek to criticise the use of trend lines. Traders should use whatever means of identifying the trend they feel most comfortable with. You will see later in this chapter that a study of the profitability of trading with point & figure charts achieved a significant increase in profitability when trading with the trend, and in that study the 45° lines were indeed used. I've even seen moving averages used to determine the trend, which may seem a little odd since point & figure charts disregard time.

It is vital to have some method of determining the trend so that one is not trapped into acting on every single point & figure signal, and trend lines are certainly a solution which many people favour.

But trend lines are not for me. Take a look at the chart of Logica which I recommended buying at 730p in The Trader column of *Investors Chronicle* of 12th October 2001. You can see that according to the trend line, Logica was in a long-term downtrend at the time.

My reasoning was pretty straightforward. Working from the top down:

1. The bounce in the market indices after the September 20th low had become pronounced, quite untypical of a bear market rally.

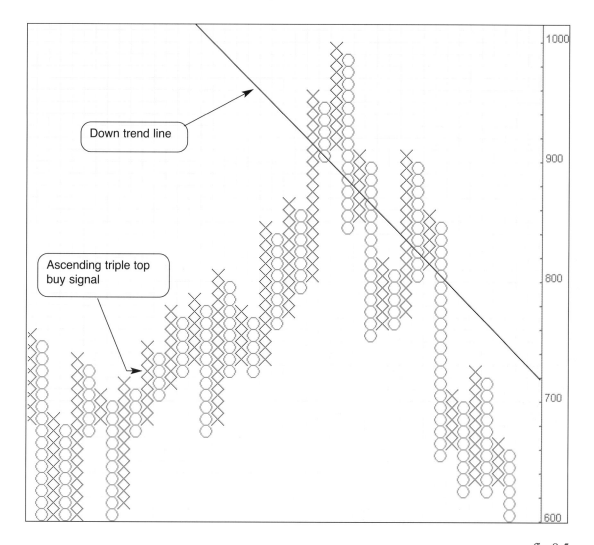

fig 8.5

2. The NASDAQ gave one of my favourite point & figure buy signals on 2nd October. However the swing chart was not terribly clear.

3. The FTSE gave an equivocal change of trend buy signal on 3rd October on its swing chart, but any doubt was resolved by a clear ascending triple top buy signal on the point & figure chart.

4. The software sector chart gave a buy signal on its swing chart on 8th October (since Logica is one of the main components of the sector index, it made the sector chart carry

less weight in my mind). In addition, also on 8th October, Logica's swing chart gave a buy signal and the point & figure chart gave the ascending triple top buy signal at 740p seen above.

5. Logica's relative strength chart against the FTSE was fairly inconclusive but it had been gaining in strength for over a week.

Not the most difficult decision I've ever had. The column sold out of Logica at 870p and 940p (two purely arbitrary levels which I had selected based on the irresistible profits which the option trade had accumulated).

You can see the trend line on the chart. This trade would have been prohibited if one mechanically applied a rule that no buy signal was to be respected if it occurred below the 45 ° trend line. Note also the irony that within a few days of Logica breaking through the trend line, apparently proclaiming itself to be in a bull market, the uptrend came to an abrupt end.

So I agree one should only trade point & figure signals with the trend. It is simply that my approach to defining what is the trend does not involve being ruled by a 45° line or any other kind of trend line. It will not surprise you to read that *I determine the trend of the market by reference to my index swing charts.*

There are two different aspects to this approach - the initiation of positions, and the holding of positions:

Initiation of positions

As a general but not inviolable rule I wait for my FTSE swing chart to turn up. Then I scour the sector indices and then the big cap stocks, looking for a recent or imminent buy signal. It is rare for me to act on a buy signal in an individual stock when the swing chart is still negative, but on occasions there may seem like a good reason for so doing. Vice versa for downtrends.

Holding of positions

Once the position has been initiated, as long as the FTSE swing chart remains in an uptrend, I will treat any sell signal given on the point & figure chart of an individual stock with utmost suspicion. Vice versa for downtrends.

You have the example above of Logica. A more extended example follows with BSkyB. What you will see is that my approach is very conservative. My approach would have resulted in 4 profitable trades in the first 10 months of 2001. If instead you had acted on every point & figure signal on the BSY chart, you would have had 7 profits and 2 losses, and you would have made more money than following my approach (but I doubt whether acting on every point & figure signal, regardless of trend, would be sensible over a longer period of time). Every trader has a different attitude to risk. You must choose the course which suits you the best.

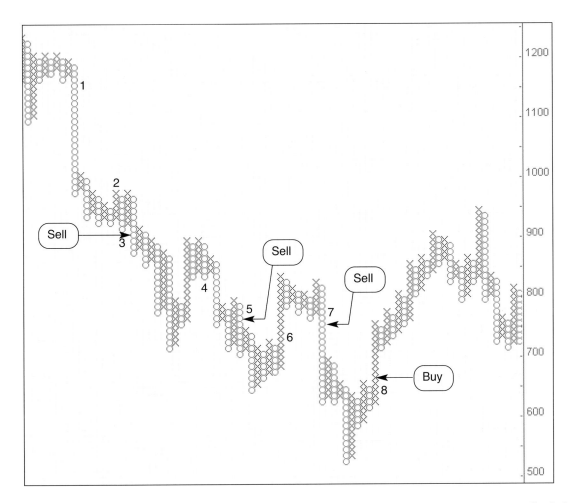

fig 8.6

1. BSY gives a spread triple bottom sell signal on 02.02.01. I would not sell short because the FTSE swing chart is still pointing up and there is no developed downtrend in BSY as yet. So that opportunity was missed. The FTSE swing chart was equivocal in early February 2001, but it turned down by the latest on 20.02.01.

2. BSY manages a small rally on 28.02.01. It looked as though a bearish signal reversed buy signal had been given. If you were acting on every signal you would have to buy at this point. But for me the FTSE swing chart is pointing down and the BSY medium term trend is firmly established. Was BSY really going to start a new uptrend in the teeth of the FTSE downtrend? Wasn't it just pausing after a steep fall? The next day it executed a 3 box reversal. Now it looked more like a bearish shakeout, which would be consistent with the FTSE swing chart. I do nothing on both occasions.

3. Another rally ensues in the first full week of March, but this is at the same time that the FTSE is working up to a potential linear phase sell signal. Significantly, BSY goes sideways at the very point that the FTSE is making its swing high, demonstrating very clear relative weakness. The FTSE sell signal occurs on Friday 9th March, and on Tuesday 13th, BSY gives a quadruple bottom sell signal. Now sell short at 900p. On 03.04.01, BSY is oversold with an RSI reading of 13.6. Take profits at 733p (18.5% in 3 weeks).

4. After a strong rally stalls, BSY gives one of my favourite sell signals on 09.05.01. But personally I wouldn't act on this. The FTSE swing chart has been pointing up since 10.04.01. Pity.

5. By 23.05.01 the position is a little different. My suspicions about BSY have been misplaced. A clear downtrend has developed and a repeat sell signal, again one of my favourites, the bearish shakeout, has been given. Although the FTSE chart has not given a sell signal, it has stalled for the third time in its attempt to take out the 6000 level. Primarily because I will be risking only 4 boxes and the shakeout is such a reliable formation, a short position can be established at 760p. By 25th June, BSY is oversold with an RSI reading of 14.6. Take profits at 642p (15.5% return in a month).

6. BSY gives an ascending triple top buy signal on 26.07.01 but by this stage the FTSE swing chart says the overall market is in a downtrend, so I would have missed this opportunity.

7. But on 04.09.01 the BSY uptrend falls apart and since the FTSE swing chart is still pointing down, sell short on the descending triple bottom with long tail at 750p. By 10.09.01, the RSI reading is 9.7. In Chapter 10 I explain that RSI readings which occur soon after buy or sell signals can be ignored, but because of the events of 11.09, I shall assume a profit would have been realized here at 688p.

8. I have already described this buy signal on page 108, which was given shortly after the FTSE swing chart turned up in October 2001.

No doubt there is a variety of ways to determine the trend. I am happy with my method, even though I miss opportunities by taking a narrow view of when I should be buying or selling. Effectively, with my narrow approach to initiating positions, and my modest profit targets, my method of trading individual equities amounts to a series of short-term raids.

Reliability of point & figure charts

Point & figure charts are effective. Having read this far, you ought to need no convincing of that.

I have already mentioned the work of Professor Robert Earl Davis of Purdue University, Indiana on page 122. He found reliability rates for various point & figure formations of 80%+ in almost all cases. I have already made the point that such high rates are not achievable in today's markets. In 1970 Professor Davis and Charles Thiel did research on commodity futures in which they found an overall profitability trade of 53%. This is more in line with my experience.

Perhaps the most valuable work done on this subject is by Dr Kermit Zieg. He started off in 1974 with commodity futures and found an overall reliability/profitability rate of 40% (number of profitable trades divided by total trades). He tried again and found a reliability rate of 41%. A third study in 1997 revealed a reliability rate of 45%. Then a study covering stocks during the period 1994-1996 found a reliability rate of 41%.

Calamity! Why have you been reading these chapters on point & figure? It's not even as reliable as tossing a coin.

Not so. The results were presented by Dr Zieg as a success. Each of his three surveys on commodity futures resulted in good profits and very handsome returns on margin employed. The survey on stocks also produced a profit although the return was a meagre 3% per annum. It still established that one didn't need a reliability rate of more than 50% to make money.

Then Dr Zieg examined the same stocks, but used trend lines to exclude short sales in an uptrend and purchases in a downtrend. The result was a jump in overall reliability to 47% and an increase in the return to 20% per annum, which is certainly not to be sniffed at.

But even these enhanced figures understate the true position in my opinion for a number of reasons.

a. Dr Zieg's method was to buy on a double top and sell on a double bottom. No other formations were considered. That is not a criticism. On the contrary, Dr Zieg's work is very valuable. Almost all technical analysis requires some interpretative skills. But if Dr Zieg used subjective interpretation, no doubt the validity of his research would have been questioned. He had to use a simple signal about which there could be no dispute. I've already made the point in Chapter 7 that I consider the double top and double bottom to be poor signals to trade with, and I believe Dr Zieg's research bears me out. Moreover you will remember Earl Blumenthal's point (see page 128) about the first double bottom in an uptrend. He regarded it as a buy signal, not a sell signal. It is the foundation of the bullish shakeout buy signal. So, part of the time that Dr Zieg's survey was recording a sell signal on a double bottom, Earl Blumenthal (and you and me) would be getting ready to buy. Indeed, for me, nearly every time there is the breach of a double bottom, I am looking for a quick reversal to buy. I am not looking to sell.

b. The surveys do not deal at all with the signals I regard as the most reliable (the triple top and its variations, the bearish signal reversed, the bullish shakeout and the obverse bearish signals).

c. The surveys do not deal with profit-enhancing techniques like doubling up in a linear phase or raising one's stop loss.

d. Dr Zieg's original surveys did not employ any optimising techniques (see below).

Optimisation

Dr Zieg's surveys were based on point & figure charts constructed in the standard way put forward by A.W. Cohen. But what would happen if you used much smaller or much bigger box sizes, and a 4 box or a 5 box reversal method (for example)? The Davis-Thiel study which had produced profitability levels of 53% was based upon the best box sizes and best reversal distances for each commodity examined. So Dr Zieg decided to explore optimisation. He used over 306 combinations (and sometime thousands of combinations) of box sizes and reversal distances in an attempt to optimise profitability by finding the best box sizes and reversal distances for a range of commodities. The results spoke with one voice. It was plain that the bigger box sizes worked best and that the 3 box reversal was still superior to any other reversal distance. The reliability rate for all the commodities considered in his second survey jumped from 41% to 66%. For a full treatment of this subject see Chapter 9 of Dr Zieg's book.

Dr Zieg's point, and I endorse it with respect, is that investors and traders should examine, not just once but on a continuous basis, which box sizes are working best for their style of investing/trading in the markets in which they are participating. Using the right box size will raise the profitability/reliability rate comfortably over 50%.

I have not made any concerted attempt to audit the reliability of the best point & figure formations for swing traders on the UK market. As a matter of impression, I would have thought that the reliability rate for most stocks is in the bracket 55-65%, and for some stocks even higher figures can be achieved.

• Moreover the whole point of being a top down type, using swing charts side by side with point & figure charts and looking at other indicators including moving averages, is to try to raise the profitability rate from the mechanically measured 55-65% rate to more like 70%. I have my doubts that a reliability rate of better than 70% is achievable over a sustained period of time.

• Even that statistic disguises a good deal. My trading experience is that a good part of one's trading year is spent grinding out miserable profits. I've not measured reliability rates but I would guess that they would be about 45-60%. Then along comes a linear phase and for 6-10 weeks, you're golden. Only by adding this golden phase to the 'grinding out' phase, does one come up with the rather misleading target statistic of 70%.

The above analysis looks at accuracy in a global way. Looking at the accuracy of individual signals, I take no account of whether the signal ultimately produces a profit. This may sound odd, but I regard the decision to take profits as entirely separate and as having no bearing on the accuracy of the original signal. I make the following, somewhat arbitrary classification.

a. If, after a point & figure signal, a security immediately reverses without moving more than 1 box, that is well documented as a bull or bear trap, effectively a false signal.

b. If, after a point & figure signal, a security moves only 2 or 3 boxes from the equilibrium and then reverses, I call that a failed signal.

c. But if the share price or index moves at least 4 boxes, I classify that as a good signal. After all, if one is using the FTSE 50 point box chart, it would mean that the FTSE had moved 200 points from the equilibrium, certainly enough for a trader to consider it a success. There would be plenty of time either to take profits or to place a stop loss at the entry level.

Tailpiece 1

I have not dealt separately with sector indices, but they are an important part of trading individual equities. Tom Dorsey makes the valid point that 80% of the risk in investing in equities is a market/sector risk. Only 20% of the risk is company specific. In other words timing one's entry into the market and picking the right sector are four times as important as picking the right company. Of these Mr Dorsey, backed up by academic studies, says that picking the right sector is the most important, accounting for nearly half the risk. One doesn't need to do anything more than study a list of the sector leaders and laggards of the FTSE in 2000 and 2001 to know that if you were invested in the right sector each year, you would have made money despite the fact that the FTSE fell markedly in each year.

I start off looking at the market indices of all the main markets, and before turning to the charts of any individual shares, I go right through the swing charts and the point & figure charts (and relative strength charts - see Chapter 10) of every FTSE sector index. Admittedly because I swing trade only the biggest stocks which have the biggest weighting in the sector indices, there is an element of duplication, so I don't want to overstress this point for swing traders. But being in the right sector is crucial and I urge you not to ignore the sector index charts.

Tailpiece 2

There is no need to embrace my conservative style of trading individual equities, but if you are not harnessing the power of a point & figure chart, I hope I've demonstrated that you're missing something.

For those who already use point & figure, keep an eye out for the shakeout especially, and also for Earl Blumenthal's high poles in a downtrend, two formations which I think are underused. Above all:

> a. Look at charts with different box sizes. When I trade the Dow I look simultaneously at a 20pt chart, a 25pt chart a 50pt chart and a 100pt chart. With individual equities I have a main chart, but I will frequently alter the box size up or down to see what that tells me.

> b. If you wait for the point & figure chart to generate a sell signal before you liquidate your long position (vice versa for short positions), I fear you may become disappointed. It is the right strategy when the market is in a violent short-term downtrend or a raging uptrend, but much of the time you will find that taking at least part of your profits early will leave you much better off (quite apart from the happy effect that regular profits will have on your confidence and resilience).

9 INTEGRATING POINT & FIGURE AND SWING CHARTS

- Integrating p&f charts and swing charts when trading indices

- Integrating p&f charts and swing charts when trading individual equities

- Tailpiece

So far I have dealt separately with swing charts in 3 chapters, and with point & figure charts in 3 chapters. I have dealt separately with the tactics I employ with each type of chart. But in real time the two are not separated - they are integrated. In Chapter 8, I explained that when I am using a point & figure chart to trade UK individual equities, it is important to determine what is the trend. Many people use trend lines or moving averages applied to the individual equity chart to tell them about the trend of that particular share.

But I swing trade only in the 50 biggest stocks, and it is rare to see such stocks have a trend which is independent of the FTSE 100 index. Indeed by definition the FTSE index trend is merely a composite of the trends of its constituents and since it is weighted by market capitalisation, the 50 biggest stocks account for about 86% of the movement of the FTSE index. It may be that an individual stock in that top 50 has the wherewithal to carve out its own trend, but I am sceptical. Since I analyse matters from the top down, I use a swing chart of the FTSE index to tell me what the overall market trend is and that is what I use as my filter to guide me when to act on, or refrain from acting on, a point & figure signal on the chart of an individual equity (rather than trend lines). As demonstrated in the last chapter, this is a conservative approach.

But guidance as to the overall market trend is far from the only way to combine the use of point & figure charts and swing charts.

Integrating p&f charts and swing charts when trading indices

When trading index options and futures, the swing chart is my main guide. Of course I look at the index point & figure charts every day (the 10pt chart, the 20/25pt chart and the (most important) 50pt chart). Generally, I initiate positions only when the swing chart gives a buy or sell signal. The point & figure chart of the index, however, comes in very handy in 3 main situations:

1. I've shown how the swing chart presentation can occasionally be equivocal, so that I am left in doubt whether the short-term trend is changing or whether the market is simply executing a complex countertrend correction. The point & figure chart often helps me resolve that doubt. A good example was the change in trend in the NASDAQ index after the September 2001 lows (see page 93).

2. Occasionally the swing chart will give a false change of trend signal which shows up as a shakeout (or triple top/bottom with a long tail). If I see a bullish shakeout on the point & figure chart shortly after the swing chart has given a sell signal, I am inclined to trust the point & figure chart because the shakeout is such a reliable chart formation, and I will at least close my short position.

3. It is quite often the case that I will use the point & figure chart to liquidate an existing position. I've already mentioned that knowing when to close out a position is one of the great unsolved puzzles for chartists. One can't always wait for an overbought or oversold condition to happen before taking profits. The point & figure chart with its ethos of reversal patterns can be an excellent tool to use.

A good example occurred in late August 2002. The swing chart of the FTSE index gave a buy signal at 4307 and, after a stutter, the market climbed up to 4466. Happily that was enough to take profits or half profits (150pt gain). But supposing the index had got up to 4450 and had then fallen back to make the formation below on the 20pt point & figure chart. You haven't taken your profits, but the market gave a clear sell signal on 20th August when the FTSE fell to 4340. Not a difficult decision to liquidate any long positions.

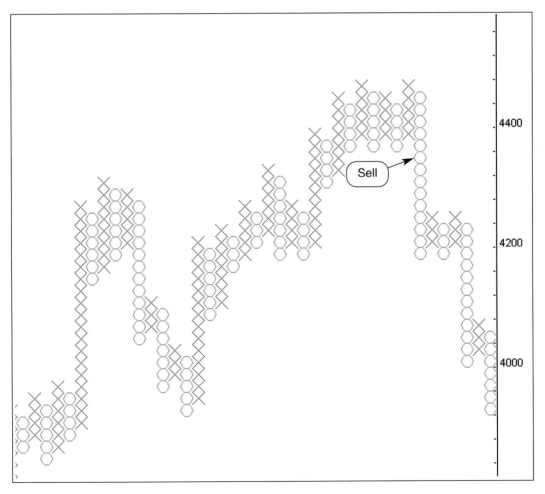

fig 9.1

153

Of course, the signals from a low box value chart such as the 20pt point & figure chart do not necessarily suggest a major move. One might expect a 100-140 point fall following the above signal (5 to 7 boxes) before the market regrouped. In fact, on this occasion, the FTSE fell over 300 points without giving any swing chart sell signal on the way, so acting on that triple bottom signal certainly would have saved a lot of money.

Effectively one can use a low box value point & figure chart to isolate points where a short-term trend may break down.

Note that although excellent use can be made of the point & figure chart, the sell signal does not occur anywhere near the top of a move. It comes only after a period of congestion results in the formation of a pattern, and then breaks down. So, in my opinion, it is not really an option to base your entire method of taking profits only when there is a point & figure sell signal, which is why I have arbitrary profit targets. The point I'm trying to make above is that in the absence of any better indication, the point & figure chart will often protect part of your profits, or limit your losses. By focusing on the relevance of congestion areas, it tells you something that the swing chart does not.

Integrating p&f charts and swing charts when trading individual equities

When trading equities, primacy is given to the point & figure chart. But I don't merely use the FTSE index swing chart for the purpose of determining the overall market trend. The swing chart of the equity is also extremely useful in 3 main situations and I never trade an equity without checking its own swing chart to see what is revealed.

a. On occasion the point & figure chart of an equity will generate a sell signal in an uptrend or a buy signal in a downtrend. Apart from looking at the index point & figure chart to see whether it too is changing trend, the swing chart of the equity may reveal that far from breaking down, the stock is in the process of completing a swing high or low, after which the main trend is likely to continue.

Look at the Barclays chart on the next page. In July 1993 Barclays was in an established uptrend when it stalled at 490p and it appeared to give one of my favourite sell signals, the descending triple bottom with falling highs, as it traded at 465p.

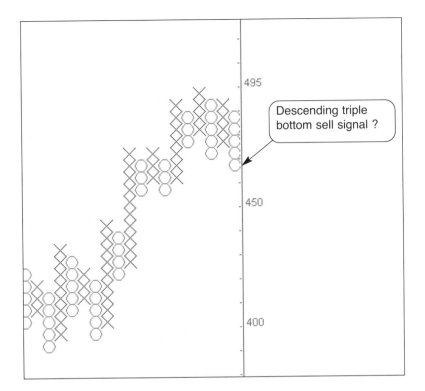

fig 9.2

Time to check the swing chart. In fact the swing chart was not bearish at all and it would take quite a lot to turn it bearish. You can see how the last clear swing low in Barclays had occurred on 7th May 1993 at 417p. The market had moved up and sideways for over 2 months. There were several occasions when there were 2 down days followed by inside days and further sideways to up movement, but there was no clear swing low after 7th May. It was overdue. When Barclays traded at 465p (the putative sell signal on the point & figure chart), it was on its third day down and it seemed much more likely that it was creating a swing low. If a new downtrend was in the offing, it would be more typical for the market to move up from the swing low and then fail. Alternatively, a breach of the support between 450-455p would give a picture of a massive top formation. So it should have been an easy decision not to act on the descending triple bottom at 465p.

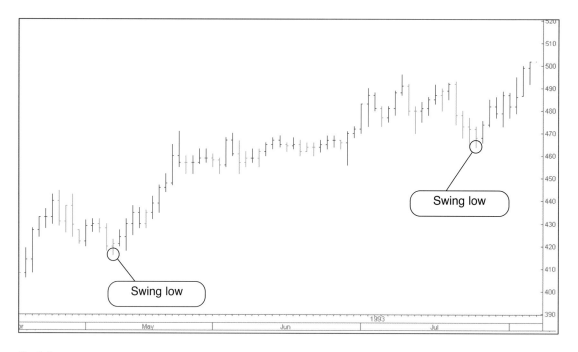

fig 9.3

That is an example of the swing chart countermanding what I would otherwise regard as a strong signal on the point & figure chart.

b. As I hope I have demonstrated, the first continuation of trend signal is the best opportunity for mechanically identifying a potential linear phase. When trading equities I am keen to take a position when the equity's swing chart gives its first continuation of trend signal even if there is no convincing signal on the point & figure chart. Of course if the point & figure actually looks negative (positive), I will not buy (sell).

c. Some traders may be sufficiently convinced by swing charts to use them as their primary chart to trade equities. The point & figure chart can provide a useful cross-reference.

Royal Bank of Scotland (RBOS) made a swing low at 1790p on 14th March 2002 (fig9.4), and after staggering up for a few days, it breached the swing lows on 25th March. This was also reflected as a breach of a double bottom on the point & figure chart. So the picture was negative, although no outright sell signal had been given on the point & figure chart.

Cross referring to the FTSE chart it was clear that the FTSE was making a swing low, not changing its trend. I mentioned this in *Investors Chronicle* at the time. So there was no indication to sell RBOS. Indeed, it was possible that if the FTSE rallied strongly off its swing lows, a bullish shakeout buy signal would be generated by the RBOS point & figure chart.

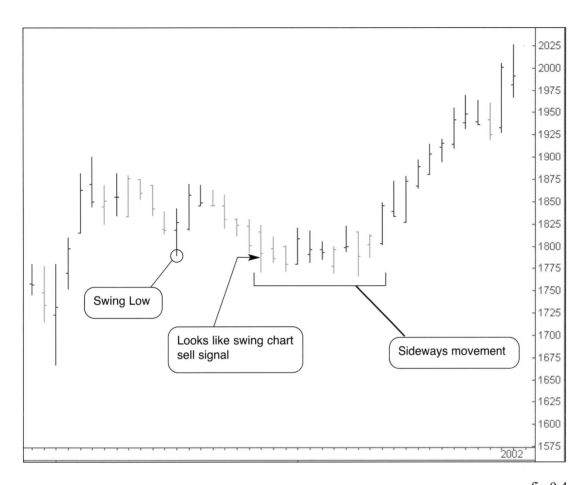

Swing Low

Looks like swing chart
sell signal

Sideways movement

fig 9.4

But on 8th April the FTSE performed a similar manouevre of staggering up a bit then flopping through its swing low. So now the FTSE swing chart was negative and the RBOS charts were negative. Time perhaps to sell RBOS? No. No bearish sell signal had been given on the 20p point & figure chart. More suspiciously, the price action since the breach of the RBOS swing low was sideways. Then on 9th April, the 10p box RBOS chart which had been definitely bearish turned around and gave a triple top buy signal as it traded through 1830p (fig9.5) . . .

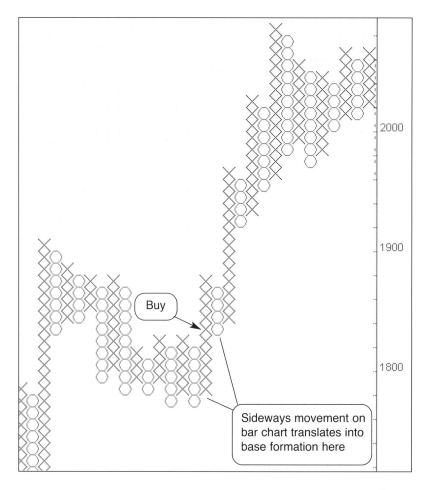

fig 9.5

. . . and the bullish shakeout buy signal, which always seemed a possibility, was in fact given on the 20p chart on the same day when RBOS traded through 1840p.

It was clear that the swing chart sell signal was a trap. RBOS roared ahead. Watching the point & figure simultaneously with the swing chart was a huge help.

In the first draft of this book, there was at this point a lengthy example of trading the software share, Sage, throughout 2001 using the full combination of point & figure integrated with swing charts as well as the RSI (which I deal with in the next chapter). But my publishers and I thought that the reader may have the charting equivalent of white line fever by this stage of the book, so the Sage example has been consigned to Appendix 3.

Tailpiece

Integrating point & figure with swing charts is an essential part of my charting technique. But as it involves so much use of judgment, because it so impressionistic, it is difficult to convey the full range of it with precision. It is impossible to lay down a set of rules. It is said that technical analysis is more of an art than a science, which I always think is a bit of a cop-out, but it is true as regards this aspect of my method. I'm afraid it is something you'll have to twiddle with yourself, perhaps in conjunction with your own favourite type of chart, to arrive at a method that suits you.

10 RSI AND OTHER INDICATORS

- An explanation of RSI

- Weekly RSI

- Other indicators

    Moving Averages
    The Coppock Indicator
    Bullish Percent charts
    Candlesticks
    Relative Strength

An explanation of RSI

RSI stands for relative strength index which is a pity since it doesn't measure relative strength, but momentum. As a result, it is always known by its acronym RSI to distinguish it from the indicator which does measure relative strength.

I use the RSI mainly for exiting positions. Knowing when to close a position is one of the most difficult parts of technical analysis. There are 3 reasons for keeping a close eye on the RSI.

    a. It tells you something other charts do not
    b. It marks market highs and lows
    c. It assists in the tricky task of taking profits

These are explained in greater detail below.

The RSI was invented by Welles Wilder. It measures the average momentum of the market over a set period. The clever part of Wilder's invention is that it is a weighted indicator. The method of calculation means that it differentiates between a 5 day fall at the top of the market and a 5 day fall at the bottom of the market.

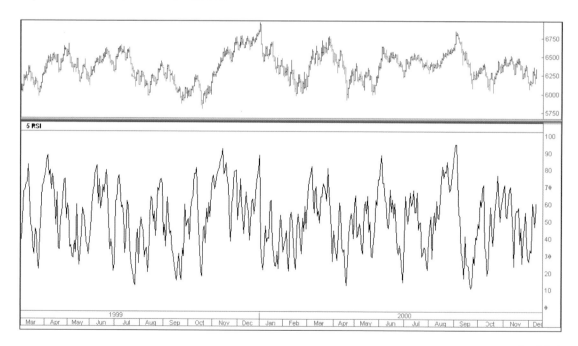

fig 10.1

You can see from the chart that the RSI oscillates between a broad upper level and a broad lower level, with infrequent incursions beyond those levels. The market or security is said to be overbought when the RSI reaches extremely high readings, and oversold when it produces extremely low readings.

What is meant by overbought/oversold?

The main thing that the RSI tells you is that the market's momentum is unsustainable. There is a clear relationship between time and price. If prices advance or decline at an unreasonably high pace, a pause becomes inevitable. Why is it inevitable?

In HG Well's *Food of the Gods*, two scientists observe that nothing in nature grows at a regular and steady pace:

> *"It was as if every living thing had to just accumulate force to grow, grew with vigour for a time and then had to wait for a space before it could go on growing again."*

The two scientists decide to eliminate the resting phase and to produce a substance which will deliver only a growing phase. They feed chicks and a baby with a substance christened 'Food of the Gods'. The chickens grow to be the size of horses. The child turns out 18 feet tall, and later 40 feet tall as an adult. It all ends in tears. Investors in technology stocks need not read the book.

So as matter of observation one sees that the markets do have resting phases. There does not appear to be a reason why a market should not advance at a steady pace of 10 points per day for say 20 days, an occurrence which would register an overbought reading near 100 on the RSI. But it does not do that. It is invariably the case that the market rushes upwards 150 points in the space of just a few days, retreats a bit, rushes up again, pauses etc., just as the two scientists in *Food of the Gods* observed.

There are several other momentum indicators, such as the overbought/oversold indicator, the momentum indicator and the market tracker. I do not suggest that the RSI is necessarily the best. It is simply the one that I use the most.

It is worth reminding yourself that the RSI and other momentum indicators do not tell you anything about value. They do not suggest that the market is overpriced or underpriced. It may indeed be overpriced because the momentum of buying has caused the market to overshoot 'true value'. But the RSI does not tell you that. It merely records the fact of overshot *momentum*.

Settings

The standard setting for the RSI on many web sites is 14 days, but I prefer a 5 or a 9 day period. I'm not sure it matters much which period you use. The RSI always oscillates between 0 and 100. For a shorter period like a 5 day RSI, a higher reading is required in order to be satisfied that the market has reached an overbought position when compared with a longer period like a 14 day RSI. As you soon as you see the RSI on a computer screen, you will see what I mean. With a 14 day RSI the upper level which indicates that the market is overbought is 70 and the lower band which indicates it is oversold is 30. With a 5 day RSI the upper level is at least 80 and the lower level at least 20.

I make the following classification for the 5 day RSI: Any reading between 80 and 88 is overbought. A reading in excess of 88 is severely overbought. Any reading between 12 and 20 is oversold. Any reading less than 12 is severely oversold.

A. The RSI tells you something new

In early September 2000, the FTSE 100 index was powering ahead. The swing chart was positive, point & figure charts of the index, of sector indices and of leading stocks were all strong. The FTSE had exceeded its Spring highs and was closing in fast on its all time highs. There was strong volume to accompany the price expansion. There was no apparent reason not to be long the market. Or so it seemed. The RSI told a different story entirely. On 31st August the RSI reading on the FTSE was 89.2, severely overbought. By 4th September the RSI reading was 94.8 - the most overbought the market had been for more than 3 years. It was an easy decision to exit the market at that point, waiting for it to pause.

There was no knowing that prices would collapse, as they did, but it was a virtual certainty that they would retrace some of the gains that they had made. Within 3 days the market had fallen 150 points, within 6 days the FTSE had given up over 430 points. The initial fall of 150 points was easy to anticipate. In fact September 2000 represented a secondary high of the 1982-1999 bull market and prices have still not regained those levels.

Likewise in late July 2002, the FTSE was more oversold on its weekly and monthly RSI than it had been for the past 17 years. It was not difficult to predict a corrective rally in August.

To my mind it is vital for a swing trader to have some sort of momentum oscillator as a guide. It is all too easy to be carried away by a market that apparently knows no bounds.

B. Significant market highs and lows are often marked by extreme RSI readings

The Dow

1996 The actual low of the year was made in January but the significant low was that of 14th July with an RSI reading of 7.6. The significant high of the year was 25th November which had an RSI reading of 95.6.

1997 The high of the year was 29th July with a reading of 87.1. The significant low of the year was after the Asian currency crash on 27th October with a reading of 10.2.

1998 The significant high was 16th July which preceded the LTCM imbroglio and the Russian debt default. There was a reading of 83.6. The lows of 1998 were marked by a reading of 6.9.

2001 The high of the year was 20th May with a reading of 87.1. The low of the year was 20th September with a reading of 3.1.

FTSE

1999 The high of the year (and all time high to date) on 30th December had a reading of 88.5. The significant low of the year was 21st September which had a reading of 15.8.

2000 As noted above the high of the year was 4th September (94.8) and the significant low of the year was 16th April when the reading was 12.5.

This seems very enlightening doesn't it? Actually it is less useful than might be supposed. You will see from an RSI chart that there are several occasions during the year when an overbought or oversold condition appears in the markets. So whilst it is true that most significant turning points in the market are marked by overbought and oversold readings, not every overbought reading marks a significant turning point. But two propositions can be derived:

> • **Every time there is an overbought or oversold reading on the RSI, you should consider the possibility that a major turning point has been reached.**

> • **When there is not an overbought or oversold reading (or there has not been one within the last 10 days or so - see the concept of divergence below), it is unlikely that the market has made a major high or low, although there is a small risk that it has done so.**

Extreme RSI readings fall into one of three main categories:

(i) Beginning of move

Shortly after the trend has changed there is a surge of buying/selling which results in the market being overbought/oversold. This is not an indication to exit one's position. It is simply a reflection of the surge of money which accompanies a perceived change in trend. This is a vital concept to understand.

A typical example occurred on 4th and 5th August 1998 when the 5 day RSI on the FTSE registered oversold readings of 12 and 13. This was plainly a reflection of the desperation of market participants to get out of the market following the Russian debt debacle. It was not suggestive of the end of a move, and indeed the FTSE carried on nearly 1000 points lower. The clue that this was not the end of a move was not hard to find. The FTSE had made new all time highs on the 19th July 1998. It had then given a sell signal. It was inconceivable that the market was signalling just a few days later that the new downtrend had already come to an end.

A variation on this category involves no change in trend. After a long sideways move (the resting phase in *Food of the Gods*) a stock gives an established buy signal, and money surges into it as a new growth phase begins. Again the clue that this sort of overbought reading is nothing to worry about lies in the fact that it comes within days of the buy signal (or sell signal, as money surges out of a stock).

(ii) Clusters

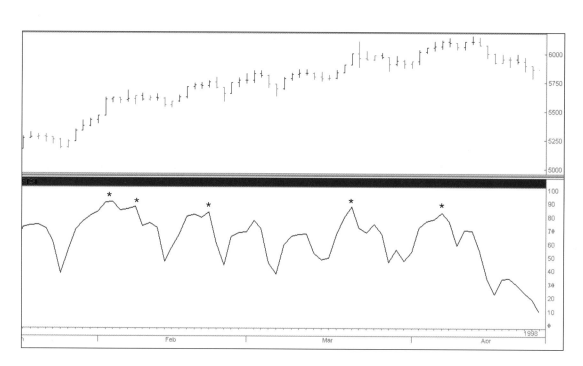

fig 10.2

Again 1998 affords a good example. On 2nd February 1998 the RSI reading was 91. The market paused for just over a week. By 12th February 1998 the RSI had fallen to 47 a neutral level. The FTSE index however had fallen less than 1% to 5553 from 5599. The fact that the overbought condition had completely corrected itself without any substantial fall in the market was a clue that the uptrend was not over.

The FTSE continued upwards and by 20th February the RSI was 84 and the FTSE was 5752. On 19th March 1998 the FTSE again reached an overbought level. This time prices were 5998 and the RSI was 87. This cluster of overbought readings was an important warning signal. A cluster of three overbought signals within 6 weeks was telling one that the market was advancing at an unsustainable pace.

Finally on 5th April 1998 when the FTSE reached 6016 there was another overbought RSI signal at 83. It was clear, and had been clear since 19th March, that the market was going to have to pause. It traded sideways for the next 3 months.

It was clusters of oversold signals in June and July 2002 which made me confident of a rally in August.

(iii) End of move

There is no formulaic way of judging whether a single overbought/oversold reading has occurred in the middle of a move or whether the market is making a significant high or low at the end of a move. One needs to use one's judgment. In broad terms once there has been a move lasting several months during which the FTSE has advanced or declined by more than 1000 points, that is an indication that the market may have reached an end stage. What one is looking for is a combination of large price movement, over a significant period of time (not just a few weeks) culminating in an overbought or oversold RSI reading. On 4th October 1998, the FTSE 5 day RSI reached 13. There had been a 3 month move lasting over 1500 points and there was every reason to suppose that an important low was being made. The same happened on 21st September 2001 when the Dow Jones recorded one of the lowest readings ever on RSI at 3.1. So even though matters looked very bleak after the terrorist attacks, the RSI was suggesting that a major turning point had been reached.

C. Taking profits

Apart from the RSI readings which occur soon after a change in trend or soon after an established buy or sell signal, every RSI signal is suggestive of at least a pause in the market or a substantial bout of profit-taking or a market turning point.

Except in the case of the RSI readings which occur soon after a change in trend or soon after an established buy or sell signal, I tend to take profits when I get a high (or low) RSI reading. My rough rule of thumb is:

Reading	Mandate
80-84 or 16-20	Discretion to take profits
84.1-88 or 12-15.9	Mandatory to take half profits; discretion to take full profits
88+ or 11.9-	Mandatory to take full profits

Of course nothing is actually mandatory, but there would have to be a convincing reason, which there usually isn't, to forbear taking profits with these sort of extreme RSI readings. Obeying this rule of thumb does involve missing out on the end of some juicy moves, but personally I find that no cause for lament. Swing trading is not a fishing contest. 'The one that got away' is a story that leaves me cold.

Divergence as a signal to exit

One of the popular ways of using the RSI is to focus on the diminishing momentum of a move even as the market makes new highs or lows.

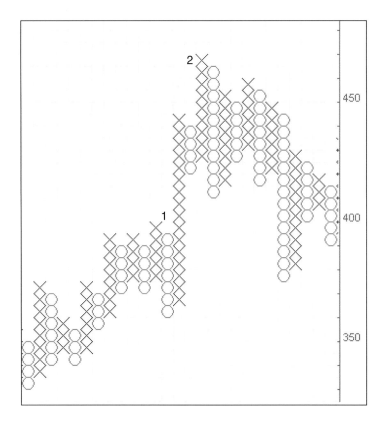

fig 10.3

In September 1992, when the bull run in Barclays commenced, there were two readings of 85 in the RSI but it was plain that this was a move that was just beginning. Those readings could be safely ignored.

1.   On 20th January 1993, one could hardly say that the move had just begun. Barclays had been in an uptrend for 4 months. But on that day it registered an RSI reading of 84.5 as it closed at 397p. Could this be a major turning point? The answer was easy. The high of the day on the 20th January was 402p. The print at 400p triggered a powerful triple top buy signal with a long tail. This was not the end of a move. It was the weight of money flowing into the stock at the start of a renewed upward move. The next day the market closed at 412p and the RSI reading was over 90, but again this could be ignored. By 26th January the RSI reading was up to 95.6 when Barclays closed at 435p. A reading this high could not be sustainable. I would have concluded that the market would have to pause. I don't know that I could have resisted taking at least half profits. A profit of 35p looks meagre but 9% in 6 days works out to a healthy annual return. The market did pause for

2 days, closing at 420p on 29th January with an RSI reading of 58. But having corrected the overbought condition Barclays rocketed to 460p by 3rd February, a move which I'm sure I would have missed in part. That peak at 460p did produce an interesting divergence.

2. Negative divergence occurs when the market price makes new highs but its momentum, as recorded by the RSI, diminishes. Once again the RSI is telling you something new. The market is losing its puff, despite the bullish appearance as it makes new highs. Barclays made new all time highs on 3rd February 1993 at 460p, but the RSI reading of 85 was nowhere near the 95 recorded on 26th January when Barclays closed at 435p. That is said to constitute negative divergence, because the RSI reading is not making a new high at the same time that the share price is making a new high. You can see that on this occasion it worked because Barclays went sideways or down for several weeks.

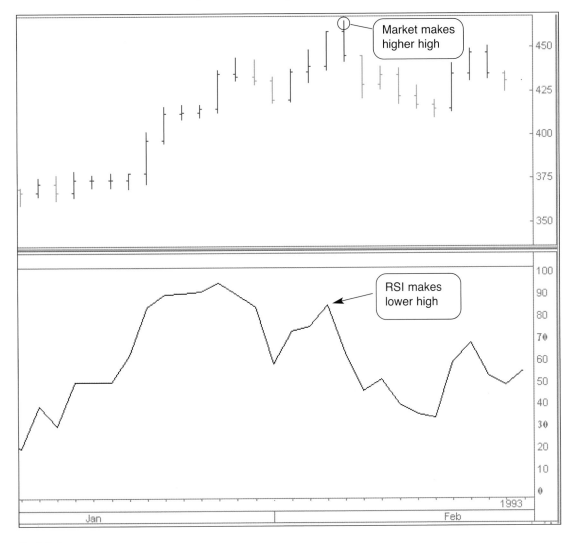

fig 10.4

One has to take care in using this tool. The momentum of a market cannot continue increasing indefinitely. Some might say that it is a statistical near certainty that the market will have negative divergence at some point. It is true that while the momentum of an upward move may diminish, that is to say the rate of advance may slow down, that does not necessarily foretell a halt in the advance. The market may or may not pause. It may keep on going up with tiny corrections, generating a host of 50-75 readings on the RSI. Not too much emphasis should be placed on divergence, but it is something that all technical analysts look out for, so you might as well be on the same page.

Weekly RSI

I use a 5 week RSI chart. It is particularly valuable. It measures the market's momentum over a medium term period. When the markets record extreme oversold or overbought readings, they will often take many weeks to correct that condition which is worth bearing in mind as a swing trader. One of the most frequent mistakes which traders make is to overweight the most recent price movement in forming opinions about what will happen next. An outstanding example was July 2002 when market commentators were forecasting Armageddon, but it was plain enough from the weekly and monthly RSI charts that the downtrend was not going to continue in the short-term. An upward correction or broad sideways movement was much more likely.

Overbought and oversold readings occur infrequently on the weekly RSI. The readings can get more extreme than on a daily indicator.

Because the 5 week RSI is a weekly measure of overshot momentum, it follows that to correct the condition, prices have to bounce/pullback over the week as a whole. One can be confident therefore that if prices move lower during the week, that move will probably not be sustained. A typical example would be Vodafone. On Friday 22nd February 2002, Vodafone's daily RSI reading was 44, having been 11 just two days earlier, so it seemed as though it had corrected its oversold condition. *But its weekly RSI was 11.3*. On Monday morning 25th February, Vodafone opened up, but was immediately sold into and went down to its swing lows at 124.25p. This was a move that was destined not to last and, sure enough, Vodafone bounced strongly the very next day and the day after, and held most of its gains throughout the week, thereby correcting the oversold condition.

The primary use I make of the weekly RSI is as a filter to prevent me from establishing positions which are unlikely to be successful because the market is oversold or overbought.

I do not initiate new short positions when the most recent weekly RSI reading is under 18, or long positions when the latest weekly RSI reading is over 82.

This is an extremely useful filter. To be clear: If I have an existing position and the weekly RSI reading is just under 20 or over 80, I will continue to run it, because it is possible for the RSI readings to get to over 90 or under 10. But to initiate a new long position when the market is overbought or a new short position when it is oversold doesn't seem sensible.

But it is not an inflexible rule. For example, suppose that after a long upward run, the FTSE made a high on a Friday which produced a mildly overbought reading (82) on the weekly RSI, and then suffered a strong bout of profit-taking, let's say 300 points, during the course of 4 consecutive down days between Monday and Thursday the following week. Assuming the sell off has not breached a swing low, the scene is set for a model swing chart buy signal if, on Friday, the market rallies through Thursday's high. And it's not going to be overbought by the close that same day, unless it rallies about 250 points which would be a very happy event, and at which point one could bag one's profits. So even though the previous Friday's RSI reading was overbought, it would not be a contraindication to acting on the buy signal I've described.

Other Indicators:

A) Moving Averages

Moving averages are beguiling. When you look at a chart it is quite easy to see that, apart from periods when the market has an extended sideways move, a trend can be quite well defined by a moving average. But using modern software one can apply an optimiser to see how trading with a moving average works out, and you will often find the results disappointing. Weighted moving averages work better. I do keep a series of front-end weighted long-term moving averages (13 week and 25 week), mainly because the smoothing effect of the moving average gives one some longer term perspective.

So for example, after the lows on 21st September 2001, long term weighted moving averages fell below the market as prices recovered and then as the recovery was sustained they started rising. That suggested to me, and I made the point in *Investors Chronicle*, that one's bias ought to be to trade from the long side. That is not to say that short-term sell signals from the swing charts or the point & figure charts should be ignored. That would represent a loss of discipline. It simply means I was more mistrustful of the short-term downtrends in that situation, more alert to move my stop loss down to or near the entry point as soon as possible, and quicker to take profits.

One often hears technical analysts talk of a moving average providing support or resistance. Strictly speaking, this cannot be true. Support and resistance, being points where the market consensus is that prices are too cheap or too expensive, do not move in line with an average of past price action. But it is not an error, it is simply shorthand. It is a way of describing the analyst's assumption. He assumes that an established uptrend will continue, and if it is to continue it will not violate the relevant moving average. In that sense, the market ought not to fall below a certain level, which, on the given assumption, is deemed to be a level of support.

There are sophisticated trading strategies using moving averages. I don't use such strategies, so I can't speak with any authority about them.

B) The Coppock Indicator

Another useful long-term indicator is the Coppock indicator. In the 1960s Edwin Coppock sought to devise an indicator which would avoid the 'madness of crowds'. He bewailed the short-termism of market sentiment. He consulted members of the Episcopalian church who told him that it takes between 11 and 14 months for human beings to adjust to bereavement or to recover from serious illness. Using this 'fact', he devised an indicator which would help signal stock market lows. I pause. Ridiculous isn't it? Is it any surprise that many investors treat technical analysts with deep suspicion?

Ah, say technical analysts, but it works, pretty well in fact. That is only a partial answer. When I traded commodities 20 years ago one of the traders would sell soybeans every time there was a full moon. I saw him the other day. I don't think it was successful. If there is no logic underlying an indicator, beware - it may stop working.

In fact there is a perfectly good reason why the Coppock indicator is a valuable tool. Over the last 30 years, periods of economic contraction have tended to be relatively short. In 1963 the editor of *Investors Chronicle* modified the indicator by basing it on weighted price changes over 12 months. Since the stock market is known to look ahead, a 12 month indicator might well provide reasonable results. Forget about recovery time from bereavement. The Coppock indicator is effectively a 12 month weighted momentum indicator.

The strength of the indicator is that it turns slowly. Markets often have secondary highs or lows. The NASDAQ peaked on the 9th March 2000, and fell steeply. But on 24th May 2000 it started a massive rally of over 1200 points or 41% in 7 weeks, and even by the end of August 2000 it was trading 38% higher than its May lows. With hindsight we know that it was a false dawn. But I don't know any chart techniques which would have kept one out of the technology market in the summer of 2000 - except for the Coppock indicator which gave a sell signal in April 2000 and gave its first buy signal at the end of November 2001.

Buying the NASDAQ at the end of November 2001 would have proved profitable for barely a few weeks. Since 9th January 2002, the NASDAQ has fallen steeply. Anyone trading the NASDAQ with the use of the Coppock indicator will be cursing. But it is a long term indicator, and it is typical for a Coppock signal to have a delayed effect. I don't use it or my proprietary long-term moving averages to initiate positions. I do find them useful to establish a bias as a backdrop to my short-term trading. Moreover, like all indicators it is not infallible, as investors have found out this year.

At the beginning of every month, *Investors Chronicle* publishes its computation of the Coppock indicator for worldwide markets.

C) Bullish Percent charts

These are point & figure charts but I deal with them here because they fit better with long-term moving averages and Coppock (from a swing trader's point of view). The books of A.W. Cohen, Michael Burke and Tom Dorsey wax lyrical about the bullish percent indices. The NYSE Bullish Percent Index was invented by A.W. Cohen. It is an analysis of the percentage of all the stocks listed on the NYSE whose charts have a bullish formation. Relevant conclusions about the state of the markets can be drawn from the charts not only of the main NYSE bullish percent chart but also from bullish percent charts of the various sector indices. For a fuller treatment of this subject, buy one of Tom Dorsey's books. Bullish percent charts are undoubtedly a valuable tool for technical analysts, although they can't be used for the sort of close timing that is needed in swing trading.

But even for swing traders, they can provide a backdrop, a bias about the overbought/oversold nature of the market which is useful. Unfortunately there is no source in the United Kingdom for such charts on local markets. I keep an eye on the bullish percent charts of the US markets which I find on www.stockcharts.com.

D) Candlesticks

Candlestick charts are very popular. At first I was deeply suspicious of a technique which had alluring names for its chart patterns such as 'dark cloud cover' and 'morning star'. It seemed to me I was being sold the wrapping rather than the content.

But there is no doubt that further useful information is imparted by the use of the opening level of a stock, and its relationship to the subsequent close which gives the dark body or the white body on a candlestick chart. Personally I don't use candlestick charts, but that's only because I have enough on my plate. There is a danger of developing 'indicatoritis' if one looks at too many indicators or different types of charts. It must surely be right to stick to a clear and straightforward method which best fits one's risk profile.

E) Relative Strength

When trading individual equities, it virtually goes without saying that the best results are going to be obtained by buying shares which are relatively strong vis-à-vis the market, and by avoiding the purchase of shares which are relatively weak vis-à-vis the market. Likewise selling short a share which is relatively weak compared to the market will be a substantial improvement on selling short a share which, though it may be declining, is relatively strong compared to the market. Most modern software has a relative strength indicator which will allow you to examine the relative strength of a share. You will notice one thing immediately when you look at a relative strength chart. Shares have periods when their relative strength waxes, and other periods when it wanes. It can be quite tricky to decide whether a share is about to end its period of relative strength/weakness. I offer no solution. One can apply trend lines or moving averages or even point & figure charts to the relative strength chart. It can also be useful to apply the RSI indicator to such a chart which will tell one when a periods of relative strength or weakness is overdone.

In the end, it seems to me that it is largely a matter of impression. I tend to assume that prevailing relative weakness or strength will continue (unless the RSI suggests otherwise). If there is a brief blip in the relative strength chart, I will ignore it. A definite change in the relative strength position of a share will become apparent eventually, although its longevity always seems to me to be open to doubt.

In the end what I really use relative strength for is to avoid buying shares which are currently relatively weak, or selling short shares which are currently relatively strong.

Conclusion

I am perfectly aware that I could have undertaken a more comprehensive treatment of other indicators, but there is a danger in a book like this of information overload.

11 TACTICS FOR LTBHs

- Limited use of swing charts

- Using options & charts to enhance returns

- Tailpiece

Limited use of swing charts

I make this brief pitch to long term buy and hold investors. Let's assume you have no interest in going short of the market. You also have no interest in trading in and out of all the various swings. There is a hybrid stance. You ought at the very least to be interested in avoiding the damage done to your holdings by bear markets. You could use the FTSE index swing chart to liquidate your long position whenever a short term downtrend is signalled (or you could hedge your long positions on the futures market). I have devised 2 plans.

Plan A

1. Sell when the swing chart signals a change of trend to the downside. Use a 2% stop.

2. Lower your stop to entry point once the market has moved 2% in your favour.

3. Re-enter the long side once your stop is hit or when the swing chart signals a change of trend to the upside.

4. Ignore any signals in December after the 7th of the month.

Plan B

1. Sell only when the swing chart signals a downward linear phase. This has the immense benefit of avoiding all the false change of trend signals, but it does also mean that you will miss part of the downward move.

2. Use a 2% stop.

3. Re-enter the long side once your stop is hit or when the swing chart signals a change of trend to the upside or after the market has gone down 15%, whichever occurs soonest. I have chosen 15% arbitrarily to try to capture most worthwhile downtrends. You could choose a different figure if you wished.

4. Ignore any signals in December after the 7th of the month.

Results

You will be better off in any year in which the market closes down, like 1994, 2000 and 2001. I trust I do not need to demonstrate this.

You will also be better off in any year which contains one substantial downtrend even if the market closes up on the year. A typical example is 1998, as set out below. The FTSE began the year at 5135 and ended it at 5941, but in the summer there was a large fall triggered by the Russian debt default and the collapse of Long Term Capital Management.

Plan A		Plan B	
24.04	Sell at 5849 Stopped out at entry point	06.05	Sell at 5971 Buy back at 6044 for 1.2% loss
12.06	Sell at 5776 Stopped out for 2% loss	30.06	Sell at 5868. Stopped out for 2% loss
24.07	Sell at 5914 Buy back at 5323 (26.10)	20.08	Sell at 5647 Buy back at 4800 (2.10)
Net	8% gain	Net	11.8% gain

These gains come *in addition* to the gains made from long term buy and hold in 1998. The FTSE went up 15.6% in 1998. By returning a further 11.8 %, Plan B enhanced returns by over 75% to 27.4%.

Long term buy and hold can be a better strategy than Plan A or Plan B. In any year in which the market has no substantial short-term downtrend, but does have a sideways trend (which usually causes small losses when using swing charts), buy and hold would be a better strategy. A good example is 1995.

Plan A		Plan B	
1) 13.01	Sell at 3018 Stopped out for 2% loss	1) 30.01	Sell at 3005 Buy back at 3025 (2.02)
2) 20.01	Sell at 3003 Stopped out at entry point	2) 03.03	Sell at 3032 Buy back at 3048 (14.03)
3) 27.02	Sell at 3014 Buy back at 3048		
4) 10.10	Sell at 3496 Stopped out for 2% loss		
Net	5.1% loss	Net	1.2% loss

fig 11.1

You can see from the chart that the FTSE went sideways for the first 2.5 months of the year. It then had a huge bull market which was brilliantly caught by the swing chart. There were multiple profitable swing trades until mid-October when the bull market stuttered and then recovered. The long term buy and hold investor was 20.4% better off at the end of 1995, but following Plan A would have left him only 15.3% better off (because of the small losses in January and October) and following Plan B would have left him only 19.2% better off.

Using options and charts to enhance returns

It isn't a secret but it might just as well be for all the use that is made by private investors of the traded options market in the UK, particularly as regards writing options. Haven't you ever gnashed your teeth at the size of the cheque you have to write out to pay an insurance premium. Why not be the one who extracts the premium? The virtues of buying options are well known and well understood by most investors. But writing options appears to intimidate many.

This section of the book does assume some knowledge of the phraseology associated with options. It intended to be purely a brief glimpse of option writing strategies. For a fuller treatment of this subject, visit www.global-investor.com/books or any other bookseller on the worldwide web and buy a book on the subject.

There are about 90 odd stocks in the UK in which there is a traded option market on LIFFE (London International Financial Futures Exchange). They mostly cover the biggest 90 companies listed on the London Stock Exchange, although there is a significant number of fallen stars left over from the technology bubble who have dropped out of the FTSE 100. Most LTBHs will have a proportion of their holdings in the blue chip stocks in which there is an option market. Each option is a contract for 1000 shares (apart from the AstraZeneca contract which is 100 shares). Each option has premiums listed for a range of prices and for 3 expiry months. The expiry months are 3 months apart. The grantor/seller/writer of an option receives the option money up front so he can earn interest on that sum whilst waiting for the option to expire or be exercised by its owner.

The two main components which influence the price of an option premium are the time left to expiry and the underlying volatility of the stock.

The following strategies should be considered:

a) Naked puts

Writing naked puts is a more cautious way of trying to catch falling knives a.k.a. buying a stock which you think has been unjustifiably bombed. By writing a naked put at or slightly below the money, the writer/grantor/seller of the put effectively takes a long position below the current market price.

It is trite that markets overshoot and undershoot fair value in the course of bull and bear markets. When a crisis unfolds, some investors want to buy put options as protection against further falls. If they get in early enough this is a sound course, but all too frequently the point at which most put options are bought is the very bottom of the market (which is why technical analysts look at the put/call ratio - see www.stockcharts.com). The unfailing usefulness of this ratio has led one American wag to describe option buyers as the "dumb money at its dumbest". It's not fair comment on the whole, but it is often seen to be true at market peaks and troughs.

The key to success with granting naked puts is to assess when the market is within about 25% of its long-term or at least intermediate term (3-4 months) lows. You could do that by fundamental analysis or by gut instinct. Or you could do it by using a chart showing the RSI. Remember though that the RSI says nothing about value. It only speaks about overshot momentum, which can be corrected by a small countertrend correction. Or you could use the long tail down point & figure chart formation shown on page 118. I remarked that I thought it was a formation that represented simply a highly risky form of bottom fishing, since one column of 3 Xs up, after (at least) 20 Os down did not seem to me to prove that any sort of bottom had been made. But that was from the point of view of the swing trader. Tom Dorsey rightly advises that you should stop yourself out if the share does make a new low. I find that shares do frequently make a slightly lower low, so I don't use the formation to swing trade.

The LTBH investor is less concerned about 'temporary' paper losses. The LTBH who grants a naked put must first have a point of view that he would like to hold the shares for the long-term and that if they spend a while under his purchase price, it is of no major concern.

The point & figure chart of Aviva is instructive.

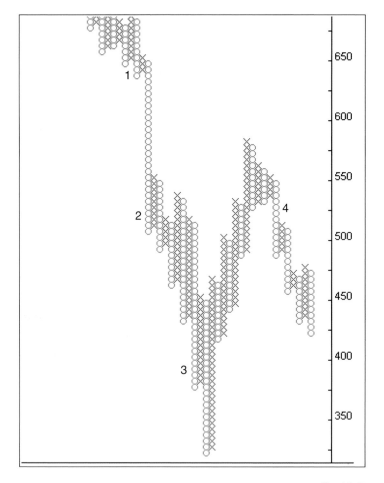

fig 11.2

1. It gave its first sell signal on 24th April 2002 at 755p, but its downtrend really gathered pace on 5th June 2002 when the FTSE crashed through 5000, suggesting that the price action of the first 5 months of the year was massive top formation. At the same time, Aviva gave a repeat sell signal at 630p.

2. Just 9 days later Aviva had fallen 20 Os, but this was far too early in the downtrend to be looking for a bottom. Short-term downtrends do not last 9 days.

3. But by 15th July there was a second long tail down and by this point it was at least possible that the market had reached a low at 375p. As Aviva reversed upwards through 390p (giving a long tail down buy signal), you could have granted the October 360 puts at 32p or even the April 2003 puts at 56p.

When granting naked puts as a proxy for going long of the market, it is best to choose the nearest expiry month, because the time value of the option erodes more rapidly as expiry approaches.

Effectively the LTBH investor would be buying Aviva at 328p if the option were later exercised (360p-32p). In fact Aviva did fall thereafter making a low of 318.5p on 24th July. It is a virtual certainty that the buyer of the option would not have exercised it. Aviva spent only 1 day below 328p, and you will often find that weeks and weeks elapse before the holder of a put option exercises it. So if the option is never exercised the LTBH investor will have earned a return of 8.8% in 3 months - an annualised return of 35%. Even if Aviva had languished below 328p for a few days and the option had been exercised, you can see from the chart what happened thereafter - plenty of scope for profits.

Provided the LTBH investor has correctly identified that the stock is within about 25% of its lows, it will not matter if the option is exercised and the stock spends a considerable time underneath his purchase price. There will be little rallies which he can use to write covered calls (see below), further lowering the net cost of purchasing the shares.

Granting naked puts is particularly appropriate in times of great market turbulence when volatility increases. That is why at the end of September 2001 and July 2002 after the market had made its lows, I recommended in *Investors Chronicle* that readers should grant naked put options. The charts had yet to give a buy signal, so I could not recommend outright purchases, but oversold readings were so extreme that some sort of a bounce was inevitable and volatility had increased so much that many option premiums were running at an annual rate of over 30%, giving investors a huge cushion.

b) Writing covered call options

This is the easiest money you'll ever make. Why there aren't legions of private investors writing covered calls I don't know. Writing a call option at a strike price somewhat above the prevailing market price gives the buyer of the option the right, but not the obligation to demand the shares from you in return for payment of that price. If you don't own the shares you have written a naked call. If you do own the shares, they cover the call option you have written.

Simple covered calls

Let's stay with the chart of Aviva. Aviva had a spectacular bounce of 81% off its July 2002 lows. Let's imagine you bought the shares for the long-term at 525p either on the way up or the way down.

4.   Then Aviva gave a sell signal as it hit 525p on 28th August 2002 (fig 11.2). The highest point of the move was 581p, and after the sell signal one could legitimately infer that there was significant resistance at 581p, and that the market consensus was that Aviva was overpriced at that level. The LTBH investor could have sold the 550 January 2003 calls at 45p as the sell signal was given.

The call options will not be exercised (broadly speaking) until Aviva rises over 595p, which would mean the market consensus had altered.

If the chart signal is an accurate reflection of the market consensus and that consensus holds until January, Aviva will languish below 595p and probably below 525p until after January. The passive LTBH will simply have to take whatever life offers. You, the proactive LTBH investor will have enhanced your returns by 8.6% over the 4.5 months by pocketing a premium of 45p (45p divided by 525p), which is equivalent to an annual rate of 23%. If Aviva falls back to the lows at 318.5p you will still of course be showing a loss, but you are the one who wanted to hold the shares for the long term. Your loss, however, will be cushioned by the 8.6% return you've already received, and come January, when the options expire worthless, you will be able to repeat the exercise.

Of course if in January 2003 -

> a. the shares are at 318.5p, you will have to wait for a rally, because the premium on selling calls at 550p or even 500p will be negligible (but the pyramiding strategy below deals with that problem too).

> b. the shares are bobbing about in the mid 400s, you will be able to keep granting 550p calls in the share, and pocketing the premium until you reach the conclusion that the bear market is over.

If you have a call option outstanding at the same time as Aviva gives a buy signal at a lower level, you buy back the call option at a profit and continue holding the shares for the long term.

Now let's see what happens if everything goes wrong. Aviva has fallen after giving the sell signal. But supposing it then regroups in the mid 400s and suddenly surges over 600p before January 2003. Suppose the chart doesn't give a clear enough buy signal to act on, or it does but you've been too preoccupied with other matters to catch the buy signal. The owner of the option will exercise the option, and call the shares off you and you will be Aviva-less. A disaster - you've made a profit of only 13.3% (595p divided by 525p), plus the interest you earned on the option premium, in less than 4.5 months (annualised rate 35%) when you could have made more (because the shares are now over 600p). If all your disasters end in annualised profits of 35%, you are going to be very rich.

Pyramiding written calls

It's all very well dealing with market prices which are more or less current. But a few LTBH investors will point out: What happens if I bought Aviva at 800p in January 2002. They may be 470p at beginning of September 2002, but if I write a covered call at 550p and the shares rise over 600p, all I've done is guarantee myself a large loss. And since there won't be any sensible market in the Aviva 800p calls, what do I do?

You could pyramid your call options provided your holding is sufficiently large (4000 shares).

This is how the pyramid works. You want to sell your Aviva shares for 850p. You are never going to take a loss however long it takes. Grant 1 contract (1000 shares) of Aviva January 2003 550 calls. If the options expire worthless, you've enhanced your returns. If Aviva rises to 550p in say November 2002, your call option will be trading at a loss. You buy the January call option at a loss and grant 2 contracts of April or October 2003 650 calls which will offset the cost of buying back your 550 call. Aviva keeps on rising. It gets up to 650p by February 2003. Fearful of having the shares called off, you buy back your 650 calls, and grant 3 contracts of January 2004 750 calls, which subsidise the cost of buying back the 650 calls. Still Aviva surges up to 750p. You buy back the 750 calls. You now grant 4 850 calls and you'd be quite happy to see the shares called off.

Supposing Aviva falters. It never gets to 750p. After getting to 650p it falls back and oscillates between 450p and 650p for years. If you didn't use the traded option market, you would look on in frustration. But, if you are pyramiding, every time the call options expire worthless you can repeat the exercise by granting more out of the money calls.

It can be done as mechanically as I've described or you could use a chart to finesse the market. Every time Aviva gives a sell signal, you sell/write/grant call options. Every time it gives a buy signal, you close your option position and watch the value of your holding increase until the next short term-sell signal appears.

Tailpiece

Since implied volatility rates are typically about 16%-18% in London (which means that at-the-money option premiums are similarly priced on an annualised basis), and nearly double that in times of crisis, the market is offering you magnificent returns in return for writing options. Patience is required. It can be something of a lengthy process, but then, as an LTBH investor, you are used to that.

There will come a time when prolonged prosperity leads to a prolonged bull market like 1982-1999 when you have to worry less about sell signals because every dip is a buying opportunity (even when it doesn't feel like it, like October 1987). But until you're convinced that such a period has started, you may think that a proactive approach to downward lurches is called for.

12 SUMMATION

- My approach - a summary

- Mistakes to avoid

- Final word

My approach - a summary

1. Look at long term indicators to determine the broad long-term trend.

2. Top down. First determine the short-term trend of the relevant market index (FTSE, Dow, NASDAQ etc.) by analysing swing charts and point & figure charts. The swing chart has primacy.

3. When trading index futures and options, the swing chart is my primary guide.

4. When trading stocks, the point & figure chart of the individual stock has primacy over its swing chart. Look at sector charts as well, and relative strength. Use FTSE swing chart as a filter (don't trade against the trend!).

5. Integrate point & figure and swing charts.

6. Use the weekly RSI as a filter. In most cases, do not establish a new long position if the weekly RSI is overbought or a new short position if the weekly RSI is oversold.

7. Be swift to protect any position by raising stop loss to entry point as soon as is reasonably sensible.

8. Freewheeling approach to taking profits. Remember Baruch. Watch the RSI.

I have covered all of these matters in detail in the preceding chapters.

Mistakes to avoid

There are plenty of errors for swing traders to make. I trust no-one makes the error of failing to activate their stop losses. Misreads are rare but they do happen. Missed opportunities through doubt or disbelief are common, but are not too damaging. They do prove why back-testing is only of limited value. My publishers are very keen for me to tell readers exactly how profitable swing trading is. It's impossible to say. It depends on the trader's discipline. It is entirely possible to make a living out of swing trading.

Five significant errors spring to mind. I stun myself when I repeat these mistakes! Is it hubris? Am I a dolt? I take comfort from the observation by Warren Buffet that there are some lessons you just need to keep relearning - a much cosier way of expressing things. Experience will mean that you seldom commit these errors, but they are very difficult to eradicate completely.

1. Licking one's wounds

W.D. Gann said there was no need to be in the market all the time. That is, of course, correct. But since trading inevitably involves making some losses, your net profit can be severely affected by halting trading after a series of bad signals. Lo and behold, the signal you decide to sit out turns out to be a successful one which only adds to your misery. The simple truth is that you have to become case-hardened to losses. Take adversity on the chin. Of course when you do make a series of losses the right thing is to scale down your trading.

2. (Over)Trying to get losses back

This mistake has cost me more money than any other. As recently as September /October 2001 I was doing a refresher course in the cost of making this error. September 11th had cost me a chunk of money, and reading the market well, I recovered some money on the oversold readings of 21st September. I waited for the big bounce which was a certainty to happen so that I could go short for a re-test of the lows. I had no preconceived views about new lows being made. In fact I rather doubted it, but it seemed a racing certainty that the market would at least move lower after the first big bounce in order to test the buying support, to make a higher low. So I shorted the market in twice the size that I would normally do, trying to get back the balance of my September 11th losses. The market didn't go down. Result: Instead of a 'normal' size loss, I had a double helping.

When you try to 'get it back' you invariably take risks that you shouldn't and it almost always works out poorly. It is difficult to be patient in an activity where instant results are a material part of the attraction.

3. Frustration with sideways market action

This is a cousin of the 'trying to get it back' error. The FTSE index in the first 4 months of 2002 moved sideways. Using my modified swing charts, the net result in the first 4 months of the year would have been a small loss. I felt the frustration as keenly as anyone. But it is a mistake to try to force the pace. Taking on more risk to compensate for months of sideways action is not healthy. It is quite normal for the swing trader to achieve nothing in terms of net profit for long periods. Sure enough a terrific downtrend unfolded in June and July.

4. Forgetting that the trend is your friend

I know there are those who use sentiment indicators to trade counter to the trend, but I virtually always trade with the trend. As set out above, my first question is: What is the broad overall trend? This determines the measure of caution with which I approach a trade. The next question, even when trading individual equities is: What is the short-term trend of the relevant market index?

This may sound obvious but you'd be amazed how often even experienced traders fail to apply it. Quite often, after a long downtrend, a market will move sideways in what appears to be an obvious basing pattern. One's intuition is that the market does not want to go down any more. A small gauge point & figure chart may confirm the impression of basing. The market then moves higher. Many traders will leap on board and buy. But if there is no reason to suppose that the main short-term trend has changed, what the trader should be doing is hoping for the market to go up, but not trading it to go up, so that he/she can re-establish a short position. It is a double punishment when you lose money by buying into a downtrend.

The error of trading counter to the trend is made because after many years of experience you'll find that your intuition is fairly reliable. And it is one of the most intellectually seductive things to do - to call a rally in the market, through sheer experience, when the majority of participants are selling. It can be a difficult fault to resist, and I confess that on occasions I have been unable to resist it. I have found that trading against the trend based on intuition and experience yields reasonable results if all you are counting is the number of winners and losers. The trouble is that because one is smart enough to know that trading against the trend is dangerous, one takes profits very quickly and the profits turn out to be tiny. When it all goes wrong, however, and your intuition is faulty or an unforeseen event overtakes the market, the losses can be large. I have never audited my countertrend trading but I am quite sure it has not served me well, apart from the charge I've got out of 'beating the market'.

In recent years, I have found a middle path. I try never to trade counter to the trend, and on those few occasions when I cannot resist the temptation, I trade just one contract, so my bottom line is hardly affected. It's pointless, I know, but everyone has their foibles.

5. Overweighting the most recent price action

It is a part of Dow theory, and a well-known market saying that the trend continues until it ends. This Zen-like truism is meant to express the durability and tenacity of the prevailing trend. But particularly during bouts of irrational exuberance or the sort of vicious falls in the markets which took place in June and July 2002, there is tendency for traders, reinforced by media headlines, to overweight the most recent price action, to their ultimate cost. You will hear absurd projections about how low or how high the market will go. Don't believe them. Be prepared for change. The history of the market shows that it unfolds in waves and that every trend has major corrections. From the point of view of the long-term buy and hold investor, these major corrections, up or down, may well be no more than a blip. But since swing trading is essentially a short-term activity, usually quite highly leveraged, getting caught by a major correction can be ruinous. Once a short-term trend has run for a number of weeks, be sceptical about its continuance.

Final word

It is not really my motive to convert anyone. The best conversions come from within. I hope I have given a snapshot of a balanced, logical and methodical way to trade the markets. But I should perhaps make a few entreaties:

a. If you've never tried index trading, give it a go. It is so much easier and less frustrating than trading individual shares. If you don't like leverage, try buying and selling ETFs.

b. If you're still unimpressed by swing charts, you are difficult to please. Paper trade them on your main market index, or on the most liquid stock that interests you. If nothing else, forget about trading all the swings as I do. See how trading just the first continuation of trend signal would have worked.

c. Although rules are good, thought is better. Think about what the chart is telling you. One of the popular charting web sites (www.futuresource.com) has a fine motto: 'The market has spoken: were you listening?'. That should be a mantra for every trader or investor.

APPENDIX 1

Construction of a point & figure chart

1. X's represent rising prices, O's represent falling prices. Each X or O represents a unit of value which is chosen by the chartist and can be altered to produce a chart which is more sensitive or less sensitive to price movement.

   In general, daytraders will use very sensitive charts i.e. those with lowest feasible unit value per box. For swing traders, I recommend a minimum box value of 0.5%, and a desirable box value of about 1-2%. Low box values of about 0.5% or slightly higher can be used for charting equity indices, but in my opinion, box values of at least 1% should be used in the case of individual equities.

2. The point & figure chart is constructed as a series of columnar reversals. It is possible to use a 1 or 2 box reversal method, but the standard, and the best way is the 3 box reversal method. With the 3 box reversal method, no reversal i.e. no new column is ever plotted until the reversal has reached the threshold of 3 full boxes.

3. Each X or O is plotted only when the exact price level has been attained or surpassed. There is no rounding up or down.

   So in a 5p box chart, where a market advances from 350p to 379p, then falls to 361p, five additional Xs will be plotted taking the column of Xs up from 350p to 375p, but 380p will not be plotted because it has not been attained. A 3 box reversal from 375p would be achieved by a fall to 360p, which one would plot by entering 3 Os in the next column. Although the share price has fallen 18p from its highs which seems like more than 3 boxes, no reversal is plotted in this case because the 4p between 375p and 379p is effectively ignored. The market will need to reverse to 360p for the reversal to be plotted.

   Suppose that the market now trades up from 361p to 377p. No new plot is made. It then trades down to 363p. Still no new plot is made. These minor oscillations are regarded by the point & figure chartist as background noise. Finally the share trades down to 358p, before rallying to 376p on the same day. Now a new column of 3 Os will be plotted to record the print at 360p, and a further new column of 3 Xs will be plotted to record the rally from 360p to 375p.

   The above price action may have taken place all in one day, or spread over 2 days or spread over a much longer period. It makes no difference to the plotting of the chart.

4.   Now change the box size to 10p and a different picture emerges. All the chart will show is 2 additional Xs to record the advance from 350p to 370p. Since no 30p reversal has occurred, there will be no column of Os until, and unless, 340p prints.

5.   Now change the box size to 3p. The first rally from 350p to 379p will result in 9 additional Xs to record the print at 377p. It will be followed by a column of 5 Os to record the fall to 362p, then another column 5 Xs to record the rally to 377p, then another column of 6 Os to record the fall to 359p, and finally a column of 5 Xs to record the rally to 374p. So the 5p box chart has 3 columns, the 10p box chart has 1 column and the 3p box chart has 5 columns. The three charts reflect the same price action like this:

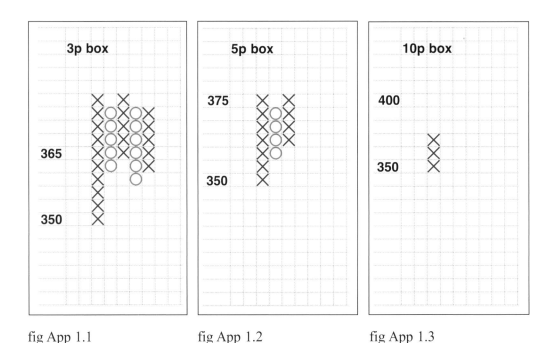

fig App 1.1   fig App 1.2   fig App 1.3

6.   **Dangers of swing trading based on signals from a point & figure chart constructed using closing prices only**

Suppose that after a long straight decline to 300p, where it closes, a share records the following price movement in the ensuing days.

Day 1 - it rallies to 312p, then falls to 298p before closing at 302p

Day 2 - it rallies to 313p, then falls to 303p, before closing at 306p

Day 3 - it rallies to 340p and closes at 340p

Now construct a 3p x3 point & figure chart. A real-time chart would show a triple top buy signal with rising lows, one of the most powerful signals there is. You would buy at 315p on day 3 and you would be showing a healthy profit.

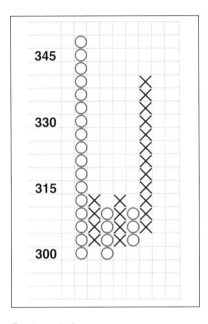

fig App 1.4

A chart constructed with closing prices would show no buy signal at all, only what looked like a bear market rally with a single column of Xs rising from 300p to 339p. So that would amount to a missed opportunity. But missed opportunities are the least of the problem. A point & figure chart based on closing prices can positively mislead you into buying (or selling) at precisely the wrong time.

Take the same example as above but change the closing prices to 309p on day 1, 300p on day 2, and then the following prices are recorded.

Day 3 - it rallies to 312p and closes at 309p

Day 4 - it rallies to 314p and then falls to 300p and closes at 300p

Day 5 - it rallies to 312p and closes at 312p

A point & figure chart constructed on closing prices would record a clear buy signal as shown in the chart on the next page (figApp 1.5).

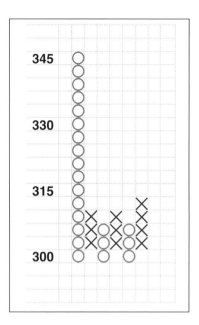

fig App 1.5

But no buy signal has in fact occurred. The market has met selling every time it has got to 312p or above. It is precisely the wrong time to be buying at 312p, right up against the resistance which has so far prevailed. You should be doing nothing, but if a gun was put to your head you'd sell, not buy at 312p. The real-time chart (fig App 1.6) shows that the market is still in a state of equilibrium.

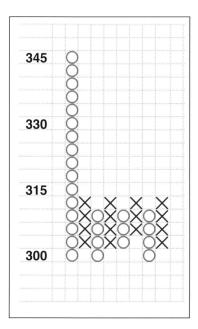

fig App 1.6

You have only to do a little trading to see how often these resistance levels hold at the top of a consolidation/equilibrium pattern. It's a potential disaster to use closing prices to construct a point & figure chart for swing trading purposes.

APPENDIX 2

Swing charting with Rio Tinto

Rio Tinto is an excellent candidate for swing trading. It is one of the 50 biggest companies listed on the London Stock Exchange, it attracts high volumes of turnover and it sufficiently volatile to have crisp, well-defined swings. I examine the period February 2000 to April 2002.

Rules

• Execute swing charting method. Stop buy and sell orders to be placed 6p above or below relevant buy or sell point (see page 46).

• Move stop loss to entry point after swing has moved 6% in your favour.

• Take profits when market has moved 11%.

• Double up in potential linear phases. Take profits on half position at 11% and on remaining half at 25% when there is an extreme RSI reading.

• Do not pyramid except when stop loss completely protects first position.

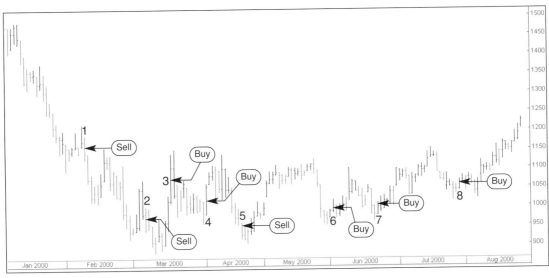

fig App 2.1

1.   8.2.00 Sell short at 1154p. **Take 11% profits** (127p) on 10.2.00.

2.   6.3.00 Sell short at 964p. Stopped out at entry point on 10.3.00.

3.   16.3.00 Buy at 1075p. Stopped out at entry point on 17.3.00.

4.   31.3.00 Buy at 1018p. Potential linear phase. **Take 11% profits** on 1 position on 7.4.00. Stopped out at entry point on other position.

5.   17.4.00 Sell short at 948p. Market does edge lower for 2 days, then has a 3 day rally which fails on 27.4.00. Don't add to losing position. The next day it trades up and the following day it gaps open above what might be a swing high. This could be a change in trend signal (with hindsight it was indeed) or a false start. It's not sufficiently clear to go long, but it is certainly enough to kill off the short position for a **loss of 80p**.

6.   1.6.00 Buy at 991p. Potential linear phase. On 8.6.00, just missed realising 11% profits on one position (by 1p). Stopped out at entry point on both positions on 19.6.00.

7.   21.6.00 Having been stopped out at entry point of linear phase position, re-establish it at 1006p, a little above the original price. **Take 11% profits** (111p) **on 13.7.00, and 217p profits** on 24.8.00 when RSI reading is 89.1.

8.   27.7.00 Buy at 1061p. Justified in adding a position here because the stop loss on the linear phase positions is at entry point so there is risk on one position only. **Take 11% profits** (117p) on 22.8.00.

fig App 2.2

9.   1.9.00 Buy at 1138p. Stopped out at entry point on 13.9.00.

10.   20.9.00 Sell short at 1090p. Ignore RSI signal of 27.9.00. Too soon after position entered.

So is the RSI signal of 29.9.00, but on this occasion it is only 11p away from the 11% target. **Take 10% profits** (109p). If fact if one had waited one could have achieved the full 11%.

11. 25.10.00 Sell short at 994p. Potential linear phase. False start. Stopped out next day at 1031p for a **loss of 37p x2=74p**.

There then follows a massive rally into 31.10. Although no change of trend signal has been given, this upward move has lasted too long and gone too far for Rio still to be in a short-term downtrend. Await developments. After a high on 7.11, Rio makes an orderly decline, reinforcing the impression that the trend has changed.

12. 23.11.00 Buy at 922p. Should be a potential linear phase, but because the trend change is not 100% certain, put on only one position. **Take 11% profits** (114p) on 5.12.00. No trading in December after 10.12.00

13. 15.1.01 Buy at 1196p. False start. Stopped out next day for **loss of 41p**.

14. 17.1.01 Buy at 1205p. False start. Stopped out next day for **loss of 57p**.

15. 19.1.01 Buy at 1211p. **Take 7.4% profits** (90p) on 12.2.01 against RSI reading of 89.6.

16. 28.2.01 Buy at 1284p. Failed. Sell at 1225p on 14.3.01 for **loss of 59p**.

17. 14.3.01 Sell short at 1225p. Stopped out at entry point on 29.3.01.

18. 2.4.01 Sell short at 1197p. Potential linear phase. Stopped out at entry point on 5.4.01.

19. 10.4.01 Buy at 1255p. **Take 11% profits** (138p) on 18.4.01.

20. 27.4.01 Buy at 1364p. Potential linear phase. Stopped out at entry point on 29.5.01.

21. 31.5.01 Buy at 1406p. Failed. **Loss of 57p**.

<u>Note</u> that at this point, 5 months of the year 2001 have passed and gross profits of only 14p have been made, not enough to cover commission charges, but that is typical of the grind that swing traders have to put up with. If you lose patience at this point, you miss the next two trades.

22. 12.6.01 Sell short at 1349p. Ignore RSI signal just 2 days after sell signal. **Take 11% profits** (148p) on 21.6.01.

23. 3.7.01 Sell short at 1268p. Potential linear phase. **Take 11% profits (139p) on one position on 24.07.01 and 157p profits** on close on the same day against RSI reading of 9.5.

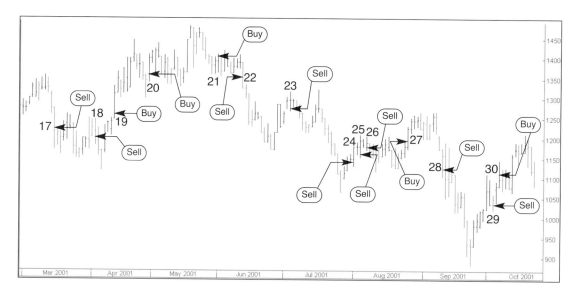

fig App 2.3

24.   31.7.01 Sell short at 1134p. False start. Stopped out next day for **loss of 34p**.

25.   2.8.01 Sell short at 1154p. False start. Stopped out same day for **loss of 42p**.

26.   6.8.01 Sell short at 1172p. Failed. Stopped out on 23.8.01 for **loss of 39p**.

27.   23.8.01 Buy at 1211p. Failed. Stopped out at 1111p on 10.9.01 for **loss of 100p**.

28.   10.9.01 Sell short at 1111p. **Take 11% profits (122p)** on 20.09.01.

29.   2.10.01 Sell short at 1029p. Potential linear phase. Stopped out for **loss of 77p x2=154p**.

30.   4.10.01 Buy at 1116p. Stopped out at entry point on 18.10.01.

fig App 2.4

31. 23.10.01 Buy at 1111p. Potential linear phase. **Take 11% profits (122p) on 13.11.01 and 170p profits** on 14.11.01 against RSI reading of 92.3.

32. 30.11.01 Buy at 1302p. Stopped out at entry point on 10.12.01. No trading in December hereafter.

33. 21.1.02 Buy at 1319p. Could be a potential linear phase, but because chart position muddied by December trading, put on only 1 position. **Take 11% profits** (145p) on 12.02.02.

34. 25.2.02 Buy at 1426p. Stopped out at entry point on 13.3.02.

35. 15.3.02 Sell short at 1389. **Take loss of 40p** on 18.3.02 because it looks like a spring trap reversal. Turns out to be a false alarm. Reinstate short position on 21.3.02 at 1384p. **Take 106p profits** on 25.4.02 against RSI reading of 13.6.

36. 4.4.02 Sell short at 1385p. Potential linear phase, but you already have one position, so add just one. **Take profits** (prematurely as it turns out) **of 107p** on 25.4.02 against RSI reading of 13.6.

Overall profit, after commissions, in the region of 62% in 26 months.

APPENDIX 3

Integrating point & figure with swing charts

I wrote an article on the software group Sage in the *Evening Standard* in early 2002, and as I pored over the chart it seemed to me to be an ideal candidate for illustrating both swing charting and point & figure principles, combined with use of the RSI. I accept that the example below is tainted by hindsight, but judge for yourself whether you think I have fudged any of the principles in this book.

There follows an example of how one might have traded Sage throughout 2001, applying the principles in this book, including cross checking between the swing charts and point & figure charts and when in doubt cross checking between the individual chart and the FTSE chart (but, for present purposes, ignoring my conservative approach of initiating a trade only if and when the FTSE index swing chart is pointing in the same direction). The integration of point & figure charts with swing charts when trading individual equities does call for the use of judgment. It is difficult to write out a fixed set of rules. With that caveat in mind, I will attempt to outline some rules:

Outline Rules

• The point & figure chart has primacy. Initiate positions on all triple top and triple bottom signals and their variations, the bullish and bearish shakeout, and the bearish and bullish signal reversed, unless countermanded by the swing chart. The swing chart does not have to agree with the point & figure chart - but it must not be diametrically opposed to the point & figure chart.

• Raise stop to entry point after Sage has moved 12% in your favour (but only on one position in linear phases).

• Look for linear phases on the swing charts for the opportunity to double up.

• Take profits on extreme RSI readings.

Sage was in a clear bear trend after heavy selling in December 2000 which caused the share price nearly to halve in one month. There were multiple low RSI reading in late December and early January. It was clear that a substantial (corrective?) rally was coming. It did after 3rd January when Alan Greenspan lowered rates.

Note: Some of the numbered items of comment below pertain only to one type of chart so in those few cases, that number does not appear on the other type of chart. It is not an error.

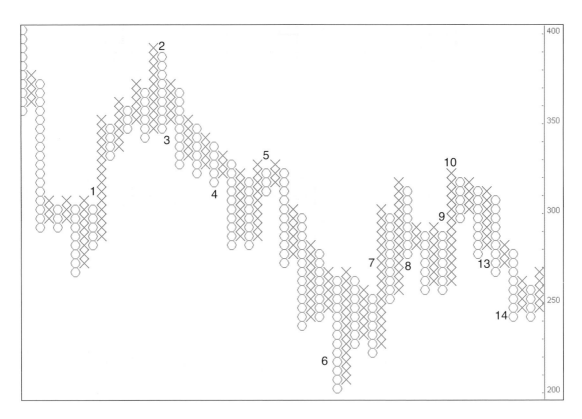

figs App 3.1 & App 3.2

1.   10.01.01 Triple top buy signal at 310p. Buy.

2.   31.01.01 RSI at 80.8 when Sage closes at 380.75. Difficult to make an objective decision here. Hindsight intrudes too much. There would have been an overwhelming temptation to take such a large profit (23% in 3 weeks). But I won't count it.

3.   8.02.01 Bullish signal reversed sell signal at 340p. **Take profits of 30p**. But the swing chart looks like it is completing a swing low, so no short position established, which unfortunately means you miss a good chunk of the downtrend.

4.   20.02.01 Still no clear signal from the swing chart but it is clear that this can't still be an uptrend when the P&F chart gives descending triple bottom sell signal. Now waiting for a rally on the swing chart to set up a potential linear phase sell signal.

5.   7/8.03.01 Rally on the swing chart, but third day up is not clear. FTSE has very clear 3 day rally, and one that suggests a linear phase. When Sage executes a bearish shakeout at 310p go short in double quantity.

6.   3.04.01 RSI reading 17.1. **Take profits of 89.25p x2 =178.5p** at 220.75p. RSI falls below 15 intraday the following day.

   At this point, you've made a return of about 65% in just over 3 months, and you think it's easy. "Mistake. Big mistake. Huge". (Julia Roberts: Pretty Woman).

7.   18.04.01 Spread triple top buy signal at 270p. Buy. Confirmed same day by swing chart buy signal. 24.04.01 Stopped out at entry point.

8.   26.04.01. Potential linear phase swing chart buy signal at 262p. Confirmed the same day by FTSE swing chart buy signal in potential linear phase. Re-establish long position at 262p in double quantity. Stopped out of one position at entry point on 9.05.01.

9.   22.05.01 Gap opening (not properly shown on this chart) triple top buy signal. But for massive gap would have added to long position.

10.   23.05.01 Negative price action. Having made a higher high than the previous rally by one box, Sage then subsides. Relevant in view of gap.

11.   1.06.01 Outside day and clear swing low established at 273p. Raise stop on remaining linear position to 270p.

12.   11.06.01 Fresh rally fails to take out old highs. Standard Dow theory weakness. Ready to go short if swing low breached even though P&F chart will only give a debatable descending triple bottom sell signal.

13.   12.06.01 Stopped out of long position for **profit of 8p** and reversed to short position at 270p.

14.   19.06.01 Oversold reading of 16.1 on RSI. Cover shorts at 245p for **profit of 25p**.

15.   25/26.06.01 3 day swing high completed, plus bearish shakeout on point & figure chart. Sell short at 250p.

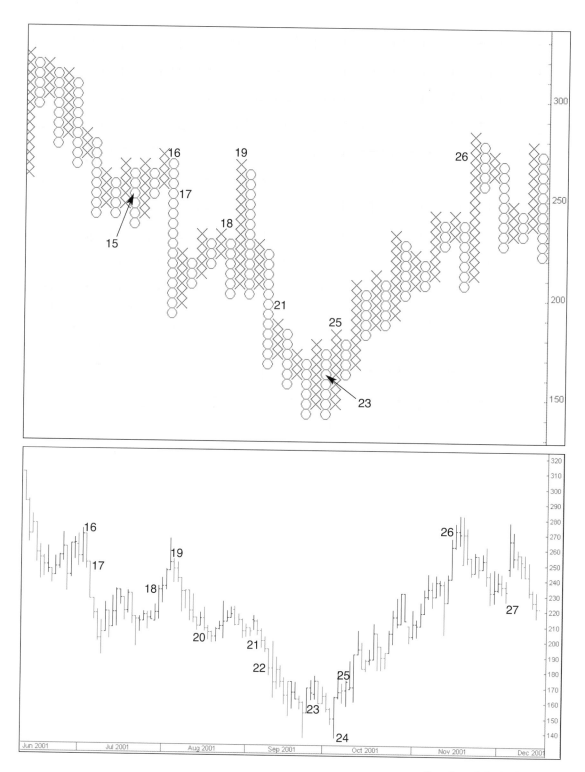

figs App 3.3 & App 3.4

16. 2.07.01 Triple top buy signal and breach of swing high. Cover shorts, but do not go long because FTSE appears to be completing a 3 day countertrend rally in a potential linear phase. This is a plain example of the swing chart countermanding an otherwise clear signal on the point & figure chart. It seldom happens, but it's useful when it does. **Loss on short position = 20p.**

17. 3.07.01 Triple top buy signal was clearly false as FTSE linear phase begins and Sage chart executes a spring trap reversal and a bull trap sell signal on the P&F chart. Reinstate shorts at 250p in double quantity.

18. 30.07.01 Triple top buy signal with long tail and breach of swing high at exactly the same point. Cover shorts at 235p for **profit of 15p x 2 = 30p** and go long at 235p.

19. 2.08.01 RSI shows overbought reading but too soon (regrettably) after buy signal to act. Stopped out of long position at entry point on 7.08.01.

20. 14.08.01 Although the swing chart suggests a linear phase buy signal, the point & figure chart has executed a high pole by falling all the way back to 210p and it is not looking remotely bullish. High poles are fairly common so it is not conclusive, but an additional negative feature is that the supposed linear phase buy signal is occurring at 207.5p well below the initial buy signal at 235p (see trading tip page 80). Follow the neutral point & figure chart and stand aside.

21. 7.09.01 Triple bottom sell signal with truncated final column and swing chart sell signal at same point. Sell short at 195p.

22. 10.09.01 Oversold reading on RSI of 15. Ordinarily this would be ignored because it comes just 1 day after the sell signal. But I'm not going to count the profits immediately after September 11 so I will assume this short position would have been covered on 10.09 at 181.25p for a **profit of 13.25p.**

23. 27.09.01 Bearish shakeout sell signal and swing chart sell signal. Establish short position at 160p but watch carefully because weekly RSI already approaching oversold (20.4) and market has already fallen 40% in less than 2 months.

24. 3.10.01 Striking double bottom on bar chart plus massive outside day. Cover short position at entry point.

25. 4.10.01 Sage gives an ascending triple top buy signal, and it breaches its swing high but it declines for the rest of the day. At this point, a real time point & figure chart would have one extra column of Xs and Os as the ascending triple top stuttered before bursting upwards I accept that a **loss of 20p** or thereabouts is likely to have been incurred before a long position was re-established on 10.10 at 185p.

26. 15.11.01 RSI overbought reading of 82.1. Take profits on long position at 272p for a **profit of 87p.**

27.   4.12.01 Although nominally a linear phase buy signal appears to be in the offing, it is somewhat late in this short-term uptrend for such a signal. The linear phase has already taken place. Sage has doubled in price in just 10 weeks. It is also December, that least reliable of months. Stand aside.

The above history is typical of the life of a swing trader. Sage had two linear phases. One was foreseen (in March), which resulted in a doubled up profitable position. One was not (in October), but still yielded good profits. Overall, there were:

- 7 profits totalling 371.75p
- 2 losses totalling 40p
- 4 scratch trades

Total net profit was 331.75p, a return of over 100% after commissions, unleveraged. Interestingly, this result could even be improved upon by disciples of Baruch (take profits early). Take the same 13 initial trades set out above, but

- take profits of 12% automatically
- ignore the RSI until a profit of 12% has been attained

Neither of the losses is avoided, but all 4 scratch trades yield a profit of 12%. The linear phase profits are much reduced but the net result is:

- 11 profits totalling 390p
- 2 losses totalling 40p
- Total net profit 350p

GLOSSARY

Back test
Apply a trading technique to past price data and/or charts to see whether the technique works and, if so, how well.

Bear squeeze
Sellers go on strike just at the very time that the bears are desperate to close out their short positions (usually because a piece of news has upset bearish expectations). Those who want to go long and the bears scramble for scarce stock, driving prices up substantially in a short space of time. It is often the cause of the bearish signal reversed point & figure signal.

Bollinger band
This indicator is named after its inventor, John Bollinger. It uses a moving average as its starting point, then plots a line above the moving average and a line below the moving average. The distance of the upper and lower lines from the moving average can be a percentage selected by the user, or one or more standard deviations. So a 21 day 7% Bollinger band will plot a 21 day moving average and a line which tracks the moving average 7% above it and another line which tracks the moving average 7% below it. If you plot the 21 day 7% Bollinger band you will find that 95% of the year's price action falls within the upper and lower lines. When the market penetrates one of the lines, it is regarded as overextended. It is yet another measure of overshot momentum.

Complex swing high/low
A correction which contains at least 3 days counter to the prevailing trend, but which has taken more than 3 days to form the high/low because there are one or more days which have interrupted the rally or pullback by moving in the direction of the main trend.

Correction
A move counter to the prevailing trend.

Down day
The market records a lower high and a lower low or equal low than the previous day.

Exchange Traded Fund (ETF)
A type of fund which has already attracted $124 billion in the US. Like an investment trust, ETFs are quoted on the stock market. They are therefore more liquid than unit trusts, as well as having a narrow spread between the bid and the offer price. However they don't have the same disadvantage as investment trusts of trading at a discount to net assets because shares are cancelled each time ETFs are sold. Arbitrage possibilities mean that the ETF share price stays closely in line with net asset value. Effectively, ETFs are low cost market and sector trackers. There is no stamp duty on ETFs.

False start

After forming a 3 day swing high or low the market appears to signal that the correction is over by reverting to the main trend. The next day, and/or the day after, it changes its mind and continues the correction by moving counter to the trend.

FTSE

FTSE International is a joint venture between the Financial Times and the London Stock Exchange which compiles a range of market indices. I use the term FTSE throughout the book as an abbreviation for the FTSE 100 index of leading companies in the UK, the most widely used measure of the UK's stock market.

Inside day

A day which has a lower high and a higher low than the previous day. On a bar chart, its daily range is therefore contained 'inside' the previous day's bar. Inside days are ignored for the purposes of counting the number of days in a swing- see the BSkyB chart on page 49. *They are not ignored completely.* Once the 3 day swing low has been completed, it may be followed by an inside day. If, on the following day, the inside day's high (low) is breached that activates the buy signal. I know this is somewhat illogical, but it is practical.

Intraday reversal

The market breaches a trend change point, apparently signalling a new trend but then during the day it reverses substantially, so that by the end of the day it looks much more like it has formed a (deviant) swing high/low rather than a change in trend.

Kagi charts

These charts are not well known but they work on very much the same underlying principle as Gann's swing charts, except that they are based only on closing prices, which I would have thought is a serious disadvantage, although I have not investigated the matter.

Linear phase

A substantial move in the market or in the price of a share. For part of the phase, prices advance or decline in a straight line without any corrections of note. The duration of linear phases are variable from 3 weeks to 16 weeks.

Momentum oscillator

The advance of the PC has seen an avalanche of arithmetical indicators for traders to use. Number-crunching is precisely what the PC is good at. There is a wide variety of momentum oscillators which can be used to judge overshot momentum. Almost all of the indicators oscillate between extremely low readings (oversold) and extremely high readings (overbought).

Not held basis
Your broker accepts an instruction which the market will not accept, such as an order to execute an option on LIFFE only if the FTSE 100 index crosses a certain point. Your broker is doing you a favour. 'Not held' means that if he misses the trade because he is busy doing other things, or more realistically, he's a little slow or late in executing the trade, you can't complain. He is not held to account for your fill.

Outside day
A day which has a higher high and a lower low than the previous day. On a bar chart, its daily range is therefore 'outside' the previous day's bar. How to count the outside day? Should it be coloured blue (an up day) or red (a down day) or a different colour entirely. To some extent the problem solves itself. Outside days are often caused by a pronounced market reaction to a piece of news. The early strength (or weakness) is completely reversed and the market usually closes near its lows (highs) of the day. As a result I count outside days as down days if the close is weak or up days if the close is strong. This is the only time the closing price is relevant on my modified swing charts, and it is only relevant because there is no better way, in my opinion, of categorizing an outside day. There is one general exception. The day that the swing high is made cannot justifiably be categorised as a down day, since it is defining the high, so an outside day which creates the swing high but closes near the lows of the day is not counted as a down day (despite the fact that the software has coloured it red). Vice versa for swing lows.

Point & figure chart
A system of plotting price movement in which the plotter disregards time and makes a new plot only when there is (predefined) relevant movement either in the existing direction or as a reversal to the existing direction. Price changes are recorded in columns of Os and Xs.

SETS (Stock Exchange Electronic Trading Service)
The electronic order book operated by the London Stock Exchange. Prices are now order driven. Anyone can pay for access to market depth information (price levels and quantities of bids and offers by market participants).

Short-term
I am not sure there is much profit in defining this term. It means different things to different people, and also different things to the same person, depending on context. The swing trader trades short-term trends. A valid short-term trend will usually last at least 5 weeks and usually not longer than 16 weeks, although it is immaterial if it does last longer.

Stop order
An order that becomes a market order when a specified level is reached. A buy stop order is placed above the market and will become a market order to buy if and only if the market rises to the level specified. A sell stop is placed below the market and will become a market order to sell if and only if the market falls to the level specified. It can be used to terminate or to initiate positions. It eliminates the need to be wedded to a computer screen on a full-time basis.

Swing high

Could theoretically refer to any intermediate high. In this book it refers to countertrend corrections. In standard Gann theory a relevant countertrend correction in a bear market, a swing high, is made by a minimum of 3 consecutive up days. In my modified system, there must be at least 3 days, but the up days needn't be consecutive. Complex swing highs will often take 5-8 days to form. Vice versa for a swing low.

Trend change point

Shorthand for the highest point of the last upward correction in a downtrend or the lowest point of the last downward correction in an uptrend. If either point is violated the trend is deemed to have changed.

Up day

The market records a higher high or equal high and a higher low than the previous day. The close is irrelevant. If you hear on television that the market fell, that is based on the closing price. It may yet have been an up day on a bar chart.